Getting
to the Other Side
of Grief

Given in memory of
Ernestine Statom
by
Jack & Billie Moseley &
Merrill & Darlene
Higgins

Sherrod Avenue
Church of Christ

August 15, 2000

Getting to the Other Side of Grief

Overcoming the Loss of a Spouse

Susan J. Zonnebelt-Smeenge, R.N., Ed.D.

& Robert C. De Vries, D.Min., Ph.D.

Baker Books

A Division of Baker Book House Co
Grand Rapids, Michigan 49516

© 1998 by Susan J. Zonnebelt-Smeenge and Robert C. De Vries

Published by Baker Books
a division of Baker Book House Company
P.O. Box 6287, Grand Rapids, MI 49516-6287

Printed in the United States of America

Library of Congress Cataloging-in-Publication Data

Zonnebelt-Smeenge, Susan J., 1948–
    Getting to the other side of grief : overcoming the loss of a spouse /
Susan J. Zonnebelt-Smeenge & Robert C. De Vries.
        p.   cm.
    Includes bibliographical references and index.
    ISBN 0-8010-5821-X (pbk.)
        1. Bereavement—Psychological aspects. 2. Bereavement—Religious
aspects—Christianity. 3. Grief. 4. Grief—Religious aspects—Christianity.
5. Loss (Psychology). 6. Spouses—Death—Psychological aspects.
I. De Vries, Robert C., 1942– . II. Title.
BF575.G7Z66 1998
155.9'37—dc21   98-27280

Unless otherwise indicated, Scripture quotations are from the HOLY BIBLE, NEW INTERNATIONAL VERSION®. NIV®. Copyright © 1973, 1978, 1984 by International Bible Society. Used by permission of Zondervan Publishing House. All rights reserved.

Scripture quotations marked KJV are from the King James Version of the Bible.

Scripture quotations marked RSV are from the Revised Standard Version of the Bible, copyright 1946, 1952, 1971 by the Division of Christian Education of the National Council of the Churches of Christ in the USA. Used by permission.

For current information about all releases from Baker Book House, visit our web site:
http://www.bakerbooks.com

In loving memory of our deceased spouses

D. Richard Smeenge
and
Charlene K. De Vries

whose living and dying taught us many things

With appreciation and dedication to our children
Sarah
and
Brian, Christine, and Carrie

and parents
Norma and Bill Zonnebelt

who make the transition with us as we enter
a new beginning in our lives

Contents

Mourning into Dancing

I should dance in God's presence, they say,
though my heart is burdened with grief.

I should revel in God's mercy, they say,
though my life is shattered with pain.

My partner has died.
This is the dark night of my soul.

Days and months press on.
Evenings and mornings lumber past.

My grief is great; my soul cries out,
"Why me, O God? Why me?"

"Not you, my child. Not you.
Your spouse has died. Not you.

I gave you life. I gave you joy.
I can give again."

Sabbath.

Rest now, and begin again.

The sun burns brighter—so slightly brighter.
The pain of the grave becomes the power of grace.

Step by step, God works his miracle.

"You shall dance again, my child.
You shall dance again."

You, O God alone, can turn
My mourning into dancing.

r. de vries

Preface

Death is not unusual. People die every day. But each death is unique. Lives woven together are now torn apart.

The death of a spouse is especially difficult. Your partner is gone. Feelings of abandonment or loss can overwhelm you. Perhaps some feelings of guilt or regret crash in. The contours of grief are unique for each person.

This book is written for those who are experiencing grief because of the death of a spouse. We are writing especially for those who have not yet retired—for younger widows and widowers. We don't mean to imply that grief is any easier for older folks. They also experience powerful feelings of loss, loneliness, and confusion and can benefit from reading this book. But younger widowed persons face additional issues, which we will address more directly.

We are writing for both widows and widowers. Gender plays a role in how one manages the grieving process because women and men often address the tasks of grief in gender-specific ways. We decided to collaborate on this book in order to examine grief from both the male and female perspectives.

We also write out of our own professional and personal experiences. Susan is a licensed clinical psychologist who faces the issues of grief and loss regularly in her practice. Bob is an ordained minister and teacher who deals with the issues of grief in the pastoral context. Both of us have experienced the death of a spouse. The writing of this book was in some measure motivated by our desire to continue our own personal journeys toward wholeness. We do not want our personal stories to dominate the book, though we also recognize the importance of these stories.

The collaboration on this book is a result of our personal grief work. After the death of Bob's wife, he wrote a series of brief meditations on grief. Though never formally published, over a thousand copies of this booklet were distributed. One of Susan's friends gave her a copy as her husband was dying. About six months later, though they had never met before, Susan wrote a note to Bob wondering if he might be interested in discussing how professional caregivers manage their personal grief while counseling others in their grief process. Following a number of discussions, we decided to write this book.

We write from a Christian perspective. We have found that our Christian faith is an essential ingredient in managing our grief in a healthy manner. This does not imply, however, that persons of other faiths cannot benefit from what we say here. Death is common to all. Grieving is a natural consequence of death, and much of what we say here can help anyone seeking to manage the grieving process.

We hope you will find this book helpful. Each chapter addresses specific issues of the grieving process from both the psychological and the spiritual perspectives. Susan is primarily responsible for those sections that deal with healthy procedures for managing the grieving process. Bob is primarily responsible for the Christian reflection on those issues. We have also addressed some of the issues of gender differences where we thought them to be important.

The primary metaphor of this book is that of a *journey*. This is not to suggest that there are stages or phases to the grief process, but rather that there are some significant landmarks along the way that help those who are widowed accomplish necessary tasks in order to move to the other side of grief.

The reader should be aware that the writing of this book was done concurrently with some of our own grief work on our journey toward healing and wholeness. As we became friends, we shared the desire to write this book. Subsequent to the resolution of much of our individual grief, we began dating and eventually married in August 1997. Although our journey eventually led to remarriage, we do not imply that this is necessarily the desired outcome for many who are widowed. We address remarriage in this book as one option, but we want you to know that there are many healthy choices for beginning a new volume in your life once the grieving is complete.

The names of those persons related to us are real and are used with their permission. In other cases, we have used pseudonyms to protect the privacy of others, although the situations are real.

We would like to thank Bill and Norma Zonnebelt (Susan's parents), Pat Cassell, R.N., M.S.W., and Art Jongsma, Ph.D., for their encouragement and support for our writing and for their reading of the original manuscript. Special appreciation for their specific comments is extended to Doug and Carol Luther (Grand Rapids Widowed Persons Services sponsors) and C. J. Weidaw, R.N., Ed.D. In addition, Susan expresses gratitude to the group of widows who joined with her in sharing their journey through grief, and for the input from members of the Grand Rapids Young Widowed Persons Services group.

1

Why Grieve?
Choosing the Journey

At 11:15 A.M. on an October Sunday morning, Bob's wife, Char, died. She had slipped into a coma around 3:00 A.M. At breakfast time, he called his three children and Char's mother to her bedside. By late morning she had passed away.

Nearly a year later, at 5:55 P.M. on a Tuesday evening, Rick, Susan's husband, died. Sarah, their only child, was detained by a flight delay while coming home from college. Susan's parents were on the way to the airport to pick up their granddaughter. Susan was home alone. Rick died quietly in her arms.

Life ends; grief begins. When a spouse dies, we really have little choice about grief. Some (usually men) pretend not to grieve, but for the most part, grief rolls over the survivor like a torrent during the days and weeks following a death.

When we ask, Why grieve? in this chapter, we are not suggesting you can ignore the onslaught of emotion, pain, and trauma that accompanies the death of a spouse. The question is, How *intentional* will you be in that process? Can you, or will you, see grieving as a process that can lead to resolution? Can you accept grieving as a process that will help you live and love again?

The Psychologist Says

Give sorrow words; the grief that does not speak knits up the o'er wrought heart and bids it break.

Shakespeare, *Macbeth*

Intentionally Grieve

One of the most important questions a widow or widower faces is, What is this grief all about? You may not be inclined to face grief that analytically, but directly addressing the reality of being widowed is necessary for your emotional and mental health. Unless the grief process is confronted courageously, you won't arrive at a healthy resolution and be able to move on. If you don't address grief directly, you run the risk of getting stuck in your grief for a long time.

You have likely heard many people say something like, "Just give it time—things will get better." You do need time, but we have observed both in clinical work and through personal experience that time alone does not heal. Moving on doesn't just happen if you take a passive attitude toward the grieving process. You must find within yourself the courage to face the pain of grief. You are going to hurt anyway; death is painful. This

book is designed to help you face that pain with purpose. We have both gone through this pain, and we
hope to encourage you to face the feelings of emptiness,
sadness, and hurt in such a way that you can work
through them in order to live a whole life again.

The Issue of Pain

Let's look more closely at this issue of pain. Some
people try not to grieve. At first it may even seem to
others that they have avoided the intense pain and brokenness of grief. They seem to move quickly back into
their lives, filling their schedules with the busyness of
daily activities, new work projects, family concerns,
dating, and possibly remarriage. They'll do almost anything to shift their focus away from the deceased spouse.
Does this work? We have rarely, if ever, seen anyone
come to a healthy resolution of grief by avoiding the
pain. Emotional pain hurts, but that doesn't mean it is
harmful. Avoidance cannot lead to a permanent, helpful solution. Are we tempted at times to run from the
pain? You bet! Grief can be so painful and overwhelming that we panic. But ultimately, we need to face the
pain in order to break through to a deeper peace.

Where does this pain come from? Grief is natural
after a loss. The sense of loss is itself a source of much
of the pain. Loss means that something or someone you
cared about is no longer there. The more you loved or
valued that person, the greater the pain. If you didn't
love and care, there would be no pain. John Bowlby, a
psychiatrist noted as a leading researcher in the field of
personality development, verified that the amount of
pain and grief are based directly on the level of attachment you had to the one who died.[1] If there were
no attachment, if there were no thoughts or feelings for

the deceased, then the death wouldn't really matter. When you read the obituaries, most of the names cause little emotional response. You don't know them; you are not attached.

However, precisely because you had deep feelings for your spouse, his or her death causes great pain. Grieving not only validates the significance of the relationship but also gives you an occasion to acknowledge the value of the person who died. C. S. Lewis, in his book *A Grief Observed*, says, "Bereavement is a universal and integral part of our experience of love. It follows death as normally as marriage follows courtship."[2] Thomas H. Holmes and Richard H. Rahe, who developed the Social Readjustment Ratings Scale to evaluate the stress associated with specific life events, consider the death of a spouse as the most disruptive stress of life.[3] You do not plan on being left without a partner; that was supposed to happen near the end of your life. Now your plans with your spouse are over—a major loss. Both of us, having gone through this experience, believed our futures had been ripped from us when our spouses died. We needed to grieve the death of our hopes and dreams before we could begin to build again.

Managing Your Pain

You must make a decision: How will you manage this pain? This is not ordinary pain. Grief is the pain of the loss combined with other emotions such as anguish, heartache, and sorrow. One widow said, "When my husband died, it was as if a great tree had fallen in the forest and left a lonesome place against the sky." Suddenly you experience a huge hole that wasn't there before. Not only is there a hole in your life, you no longer feel whole. A piece of you is missing.

A common reaction to the death of your spouse is to feel that part of you died. And it is true that part of you did die—the part that was defined by the relationship with your spouse. But with time and work, you will realize that *you* did not die. You are whole and complete in yourself. One is a whole number, you know. The grieving process allows you to adjust to an environment that has changed, to let the wound heal, and to get on with your life.

Getting on is not easy. Death creates a myriad of thoughts and feelings that simply cannot be stored away. Feelings are spontaneous reactions to the things about which we think. Many people have been taught to suppress and distrust their feelings. But feelings are neither right nor wrong. You experience feelings like the wind in your face. They just are, and they need to be viewed as a normal condition regardless of your circumstance.

Feelings can be stored for a little while but not very long. When your child scores the crucial point in a ball game, you don't wait a few days before you holler and shout. You scream at that moment. The same is true for negative feelings. We can temporarily avoid dealing with our feelings, but we have only a limited storage space for those feelings. Once that space is full, the feelings have no place to go. When feelings are suppressed, they may surface later in a context that doesn't fit the emotion. This may cause confusion, overreaction, or other forms of unhealthy disruption. Or the feelings may come back as headaches, stomach problems, medical disorders, or depression. Dealing with feelings *now* rather than later is a healthier choice. Experiencing the thoughts and feelings of grief will move you into unknown territory, but you need to go into the pain if you want to get to the other side of grief.

The Other Side of Grief

Grief does have another side. You can celebrate the positive result of grieving. That may sound strange or even repulsive to someone in the early phases of grief. Are we suggesting that grieving itself should be celebrated? Certainly not. Grieving is a tedious, unpleasant, and lonely process earmarked by immense pain. But you can celebrate the new optimism and perspective on life that grieving can bring. Grieving is a journey through a frightening land in order for you to discover a new life with some exciting possibilities on the other side of grief. Hang on to that thought!

The major problem widowed persons have is that they do not typically choose pain; they try to avoid it. Most of us have been taught that grief is something to endure, something to put up with. If we just hang in there, life will get better. But we want to encourage a different approach: Don't avoid the pain—attack it. Don't endure the grief—manage it.

Choosing to grieve is a necessary component to a full and healthy resolution of grief. Getting to the other side of grief doesn't happen without the pain and heartache. This first chapter is a challenge to take charge and to find the courage to choose to do grief work. Loss changes us, but don't let the death of your spouse kill your own spirit. Grief can be the occasion to make positive changes such as awakening a compassionate heart or establishing a new set of priorities.

Perhaps you've seen the poster with a cat out on a limb. The caption reads: "Some say you're strong to hold on. But sometimes you're stronger if you let go!" When your spouse dies, the tendency is to hang on. At the beginning, hanging on is probably the only thing you can do, but you know you can't stay on that limb forever. You can't grieve for the rest of your life;

you must learn to let go. Like the toddler taking his or her first steps, we finally have to let go in order to get going. Grieving is a journey that can have a positive resolution.

So what is resolution of grief, and what does it mean for those of us who are widowed? I have heard some widowed persons say, "You never get over it!" or, "The pain is always there." We disagree. That sounds like a death sentence for the survivor. We think it is possible to get to a place where you no longer feel pain at the mention of your spouse's name. The powerful longing for the person's presence in your life can fade and finally disappear. You can retain all your memories or think with deep fondness of this important person who was in your life. You may experience powerful emotions on occasions like your wedding anniversary, graduations, weddings, or the birth of grandchildren. These milestones can be occasions to revisit your grief, but pain doesn't have to be there. Instead, you may feel sadness or regret that your spouse can't see the event—the culmination of a successful past. Yet, you did not die; your life is not over. You can move on, creating new shapes and forms for your life. Life is still in front of you to discover and experience.

Look at it this way: Life is a journey. You want to experience every part of that journey fully, but you also don't want to stop at one place too long. The journey must continue. Most of us do not regret that our childhood is over. You probably enjoyed those years, but you have moved on. You wouldn't want to be fourteen years old for the rest of your life; you looked forward to adulthood.

So also with the death of a spouse; you need to move on. You had the experience of your marriage (like other past experiences), but you must not settle down and stop the journey. Your marriage is over because of the death of your spouse, but your life isn't. A volume may be concluded, but your life isn't over. Without managing your grief process intentionally, you may create more problems for yourself than what grief itself gave you. Why not deal with the feelings and emotions related to grief so that the next step in your journey can be as free of the previous baggage as possible? Grief can be changed from pain to hope and from hope to a deeper life. John Greenleaf Whittier was, in a sense, speaking of unresolved grief when he said, "For of all sad words of tongue or pen, the saddest are these: it might have been."[4] You know the sensation. You may feel like you are only existing. Be careful. Do not waste the rest of your life on what "might have been." Deal with the grief. Deal with it now so that you can get on with your life.

The Pastor Says

We do not want you to be ignorant about those who fall asleep, or to grieve like the rest of men, who have no hope.

1 Thessalonians 4:13

The Grieving Christian

"Until death do us part." We gloss over the words quickly at the wedding. After all, a wedding is a sign of new life. We really don't want to talk about death in the middle of a celebration of new life.

But then the word comes: "The growth is massive; something is seriously wrong." Or, "I'm sorry—the seizure was caused by a tumor pressing on the brain." Others hear the message from the state police: "Mrs. Mitchell, I am sorry to inform you that your husband has been killed in an accident on the expressway. Please come with me." The journey begins. No slow, gentle acceleration. An avalanche of shock, terror, and pain engulfs you. One minute your life is routine; the next minute you stare death in the face.

Let's be clear at the outset: God doesn't want people to die; he created them to live. Not only were we created to live, we were created to be together, with marriage the most intimate human relationship. The beautiful relationship of God the Father, God the Son, and God the Spirit is reflected in the union of a man and woman (Gen. 1:27). Paul uses marriage as a symbol of the close bond between Christ and his body (Eph. 5:25–33).

Then death comes to end the marriage relationship. That should be no surprise, but death rarely comes when we want it to. Death comes too early or too late, and grief is always death's traveling companion.

Attack the Myths

An especially harmful myth held by some Christians is that God doesn't want us to grieve. People won't say it directly, but many of their comments lead us to believe Christians really shouldn't grieve a spouse's death too much. "After all," they say, "your spouse is better off now. And God will make it all right," insinuating that we should not cry.

The real question most of us face at the beginning of the grieving process is this: Is it okay for me as a Christian to wail? Not just to weep or cry a little at socially acceptable times, but to wail? I want to scream. I want to cry out. But are such emotions a sign of a weak faith? Does it mean I really don't trust God enough? What if I come home the first night after visitation at the funeral home and am so angry I smash a vase against the wall, leaving the pieces for someone else to pick up? Does this mean my faith has failed?

We believe God understands these feelings. "Jesus wept" (John 11:35) is the shortest verse in the Bible. Look at the treasure hidden in those two words. Jesus—the very Lord of Life, the King of Kings—is on his knees before the tomb of Lazarus, his dear friend. And he weeps. Why? Certainly not because Lazarus is dead. Jesus will, within the next few minutes, call him back to life. Lazarus will come storming from the tomb. Death can't hold him back with the power of Christ on his side. Jesus is weeping because sin has broken this world, and death is a symbol of that brokenness. Even though he has the power to fix it, Jesus grieves.

We also have the freedom to grieve. Death is not the way it's supposed to be. Death is unnatural. Death is an intrusion. And even though Christ has ultimately conquered death, we still face it. And we weep.

We need to deal with several important issues in order to gain a Christian perspective on grief. When your spouse dies, you grieve for at least three different reasons: loss of a spouse, loss of control, and disappointment with God.

1. *Loss of a spouse.* Your spouse complemented you; he or she was your soul mate. That's what God intended from the very beginning of creation. Adam and Eve were meant to be together—to be soul mates. They came alongside each other as partners in life.

A married couple weaves their lives together into a beautiful tapestry. Ideally, each retains his or her own individuality and personality. The individual threads are visible, distinctive, and contribute to the strength of the relationship, but they are woven together. You cannot remove one strand without exacting a great price from the rest. The death of a spouse at any age triggers an unraveling process, and that hurts. For younger widowed persons the pain can be all the greater because the final pattern of their tapestry has not fully developed. While retired folk still grow and develop together, their marriage usually has a certain wholeness and integrity. Younger couples are still under construction. Calling this an untimely death simply confirms that the final pattern is not yet complete.

Some people may do theological gymnastics to justify an untimely death. "It's in God's plan," they will say. But death is foreign to God. He never intended it—at least not the pain, sorrow, and suffering that goes with it. Certainly death has been conquered in Christ, but that doesn't mean we cannot, may not, or should not wail in its presence.

2. *Loss of control.* We grieve because we are confronted with a powerful reminder that we are not in control. If your spouse died after a lengthy illness, you likely have already faced the issue of control. You can't control doctors' schedules. You certainly can't control the outcome of lab tests. As hard as you may have tried, you may now face a powerful sense of failure because you could not control the situation. Your spouse died. You are alone.

But you never were in control. God is. Strange as this may sound, you can't even control your own faith. I had taken this business of waiting on the Lord and made it into my job. I would say, "This is my duty. My job is to wait. I will pour my faith into the waiting, and we will see how well I can do this waiting business." But still nothing happened, and finally I had to learn that the strength of my faith did not depend solely on me but also on others. The body of Christ is *not* made up of strong parts and weak parts, with the strong parts supporting the weak. The body is composed of weak parts—all of them. We each come to the body with our own hurts, pains, and weaknesses. Weak parts must hold up other weak parts. Death is a cruel but unavoidable reminder that I am not in control of anything—not even my faith.

3. *Disappointment with God.* If I am not in control, then (so we argue) God surely is. And God is merciful, loving, and kind. God brought us together in this beautiful union, so how can a loving God allow this to happen? You are disappointed in God; you may even be angry with him. You may wonder if you can really trust him again. There are no easy answers, so you want to grab God by the collar, shake him, and demand an explanation. But God may not answer. The only answer you may receive at that moment is that there is no explanation. At its very nature death is demonic, and you cannot explain the demonic. Death happens. It is not really God's fault, nor yours, nor that of your spouse. Death is the devil's calling card.

So you grieve. You grieve the loss of your spouse. You grieve the loss of control. You grieve a God who doesn't always answer your questions. What you see and understand now is "but a poor reflection as in a mirror. . . . Now I know in part; then I shall know fully, even as I am fully known" (1 Cor. 13:12).

One of my pastors and a close personal friend stated it well: "Grief is a necessary process. When your spouse dies, you can't avoid it. But remember, it is a process. And with every process, there is a goal. Go ahead—

grieve. Grieve heartily. Grieve so that you can live and love again."

Once you have debunked the myth that God doesn't want us to grieve, go on to attack the myths that death is God's fault, that God does not understand, and that you will never be happy again.

1. *Death is not God's fault.* God's entire purpose in sending his Son was to overcome death. The cross was the decisive battle, and the outcome of the battle is already guaranteed, but the war wages on. Only when Christ comes again will the victory be complete. So you grieve—but not like others. For while you can wail and weep, you also have the hope of the resurrection. Death is real; death is painful. But "I am convinced that neither death nor life . . . will be able to separate us from the love of God that is in Christ Jesus our Lord" (Rom. 8:38–39).

2. *God does understand.* He is not so high and mighty that he doesn't grieve with us. The Spirit of God groans with us in our pain (Rom. 8:26). Jesus wept. He also experienced death when he "humbled himself and became obedient to death—even death on a cross!" (Phil. 2:8). More importantly, Jesus challenged death and the grave—and he won.

3. *You can be happy again.* Don't believe the myth that you will never be happy again. If your spouse died recently, this may be difficult to understand or accept, but God does restore. God, in his own way, returns happiness. This happiness may come in many other forms. Your life will probably never be what you had imagined it to be, but God can open new doors. God doesn't promise that he will do for everyone what he did for Job, who was so severely afflicted that he lost all his earthly possessions, his health, and all his children. But

in the end, "The LORD blessed the latter part of Job's life more than the first" (Job 42:12).

We must believe that God wants good things for us. Evil cannot and must not prevail. Allow for the possibility that you will be happy again. God is gracious.

2

How Do You Grieve?

Mapping the Route from Pain to Memories

Harold's wife died, and for years he kept a box filled with special mementos to remind him of his past love. He had taken her watch, a few pieces of sentimental jewelry, some pictures, a small bottle of her favorite perfume, and other assorted treasures and sealed them in a box. From time to time Harold would move the box from one room to another, putting it in a closet or under a bed, making certain it was in a secure place. But Harold never opened the box.

How will you grieve? Will you carry your memories in a sealed container, never daring to look inside? Or will you open the box, face the memories, and learn to relish the pleasure they can bring? In this chapter we will suggest how to turn your present pain of grief into a treasure house of beautiful memories.

The Psychologist Says

No one cries very much unless something of real worth is lost. So grieving is a celebration of the depth of the union. Tears are the jewels of remembrance—sad, but glistening with the beauty of the past.

James Peterson,
"On Being Alone," *The Adventist Chaplain*

Tears won't bring him back, but they might bring you back.

Barbra Streisand in *Prince of Tides*

Facing the Emotional Pain—
Not around or over but through It

We all want to avoid pain, especially physical pain. When you twist your back and it hurts, you immediately quit what you're doing. A child who touches a hot stove jerks back because of the pain. Avoiding physical pain is normal and healthy.

Emotional pain is different, however. Because emotional pain consists of a myriad of feelings such as fear, anger, guilt, and sadness, you need to identify and explore those feelings.

C. S. Lewis says, "No one ever told me that grief felt so much like fear. I am not afraid, but the sensation is like being afraid. The same fluttering stomach, the same restlessness, the yawning. I keep on swallowing."[1]

You cannot avoid reacting to your grief. You probably have already experienced the shock, numbness, and disbelief that came with your spouse's death. The bottom probably fell out of your world. You may have experienced

changes in your sleeping or eating patterns. Your emotions may be fragile; you may even think you're going
crazy. These feelings may scare you, and you may try to
deny them. You want to get control of the situation, so
you try not to cry, express anger, or feel guilty. You may
not feel like going to church or socializing with friends,
but the pressure to fit in is so great that you pretend you're
doing okay, and you go out anyway. Do yourself a favor—
stop the acting. It will be harmful to you later.

Widowhood happens to half of all married people. One
person in every couple will die and leave the other widowed. You may think you are in the minority. However,
eight hundred thousand individuals face the stark reality
of their spouse's death annually. About one-fourth of them
are men; the other three-fourths are women. The United
States Census Bureau indicates that 7 percent of the
United States population is widowed. About four hundred thousand of those widowed are under the age of forty-
five, and 6.1 million persons are between the ages of forty-
five and sixty. Of the persons over the age of sixty-five,
50 percent of the women and 14 percent of the men are
widowed. In other words, you are not alone.

Because we will all die, widowhood is something that
one partner in every marriage will face. You usually do
not think of death at the marriage altar, although the
words "until death do us part" are fairly standard in the
wedding ceremony.

What Is Grief?

Grief consists of the thoughts and feelings as well as
the psychological, social, physical, and spiritual reactions we experience with the death of a loved one.
Grieving is an individual, unique process. There is no
right way to grieve, so you need to give yourself per-

mission to grieve in your own way and at your own pace. But those who grieve do have some common experiences. We encourage you to look at each of them to understand what you are experiencing. As you grieve, look within yourself, befriend yourself, and know how you are doing.

The three most common factors that affect the grieving process are: (1) the nature and characteristics of the relationship you had with the deceased, (2) your personality characteristics related to your personal circumstances, and (3) the type of death. We will spend some time considering each of these in some detail.

Your Relationship with the Deceased

The type of relationship you had with your spouse is an important factor in understanding the grieving process. The quality of your marital relationship, how close you were to your spouse, and what roles you played in that union will make a difference in your grieving. Obviously, the closer you were to your spouse, the more you will have to restructure your life. If you had some unresolved conflict or major disagreements with your deceased spouse, you will likely experience more complications. Naturally, no marital relationship is perfect, but if a consistent or pervasive problem existed between you, you need to resolve not only the grief but the conflict as well. We suggest that if this describes your situation, you seek a counselor to help sort through these issues. Mental health professionals generally agree that grieving will be less complicated when the marital relationship was healthy.

Your Personality Characteristics Related to Your Personal Circumstances

Your own personal circumstances also affect the grieving process. Actually, this category covers a number of factors such as your previous experiences with death, personality type, education and employment status, health, financial situation, family responsibilities, social support, and presence of religious beliefs.

For example, the more financially stable you were prior to the death of your spouse, the less traumatic your life will likely be when widowed. As crass as it may seem, you still have to think about money during your period of grief. Wise decisions need to be made about money matters. Inadequate financial resources create distress. If you are established in your own career or have fulfilling employment, you have an asset in approaching the grief process. Work can serve as an excellent distraction by reminding you that your life is more than the marriage. However, you can overdo it. Don't bury yourself in work to avoid dealing with the death of your spouse. But if your work provides a sense of satisfaction and fulfillment, go ahead and work. In most cases, working can help maintain self-esteem. Part of your identity is gone with the death of your spouse, but that identity wasn't all of you because you are a valuable person. You still exist. Begin now to do what you can to rebuild your own sense of self-worth.

How you have dealt with previous losses is also significant. If you are a survivor of a previous loss, you know you made it through once. Each time you make it through you can become stronger. But this strength will come only if you dealt with the prior losses in a healthy manner. If you avoided working through the grief then, you will probably find this new grief even harder to handle because the earlier experiences will also resurface, complicating your bereavement.

Your own personality also has a profound impact on your grieving. Some of us tend to be primarily thinkers, wanting to understand everything. Others are feelers,

responding more often emotionally to our circumstances. The healthiest perspective is one that main-
tains a balance between thinking and feeling.

Another personality trait that affects the grieving
process is pessimism or optimism. If you tended to look
primarily at the negative factors in any given situation
and focus on them, it will be more difficult to allow
yourself eventually to work toward accepting your
spouse's death and finding present and future positive
results. You may have heard the old adage, If you are
given a lemon, make lemonade. That could certainly
apply at some point in your grief work, but don't rush
too quickly to "make lemonade." It is important to experience and deal with all your feelings (e.g., anger, sadness, guilt) before moving on. If you were an optimistic
and positive person prior to your spouse's death, you
will likely be able to recapture that attitude again.

Your own physical health may also affect the grieving process. If you are in poor health or lack energy, you
may discover that your grieving process will take longer.
You may also develop a deeper appreciation for your own
health, as I did. Rick had been ill for a very long time
prior to his death, so now having the energy to do what
I want to physically is extremely important for me.

Another personal circumstance that influences the
grieving process is your own family history and dynamics. If you have children at home, for example, you
obviously will need to care for them. You may find it
necessary, at times, to put your own feelings and needs
on the shelf in order to attend to your kids. Little children can present a special challenge since they are so
physically dependent on parents. While it is one thing
to meet their physical needs, you also will want to meet
their emotional needs. You may feel torn because you
do not feel emotionally equipped to deal with your chil-

dren's needs at the same time you are dealing with your own grief.

Under normal circumstances, it was an ordinary routine for Jennifer to get her daughter dressed and ready for school. Even if her daughter resisted, Jennifer would have the emotional stability to handle it. But as a widow of five months, Jennifer often found herself emotionally strung out and teary in the morning about the loss of her spouse when simultaneously her six-year-old would be refusing to get ready for school.

Life's challenges don't wait to present themselves until you are ready to handle them. Grief forces us to choose sometimes, even on the emotional level. Your needs and your child's needs may often present themselves concurrently and create a conflict. Frequently the child's needs appropriately win out. This, in some ways, postpones your grieving until you can return to it later. Parents, siblings, and other family members can help you handle some of your children's needs. This help can be invaluable if they are sensitive to your desires and wishes. You will have to set clear boundaries about what you want them to do and how much you will still do yourself.

Religious beliefs can also be a complicating factor in the grief process. Bob and I are both Christians, and we know that our faith in God and trust in his care can be very reassuring. However, the grief process invariably throws the question in your face, Why, God, did you allow this to happen to me? Why, indeed! Some folks may immediately feel guilty for even asking the question. Or you may find yourself becoming extremely angry at God, feeling deserted by him, or even wondering if he is still there. You may choose not to pray, attend church, or have devotions. If you are experiencing that now, remember that such a reaction is normal and it will eventually pass. Give yourself permission to experience this dark night of the soul without feeling guilty. As you continue in your grief process, your faith will help you come to life again, understanding that life intertwines joy and sorrow.

Social expectations also affect the way you grieve. Many people will judge how well you are doing by some unspoken standard. Well-meaning family or friends probably want you to be back to your old self, encouraging you to stop moping around. But they may not know what it is like to lose a spouse. Or they may be reacting to their own anxiety in handling your loss and the subsequent social changes. Regardless of their motivation, their expectations can add to your burden. You are already alone; not being understood by others only makes you feel more alienated. If you and your spouse had a very special kinship, not being able to share your feelings with anyone else now only intensifies your pain and sense of loss.

Experiencing the firsts without your spouse is extremely difficult, so don't let other people's expectations influence you. The only right timing for you is found by listening to and following your heart. Completing the grieving process within a year is highly unlikely. The intensity of the grief may begin to subside, the waves of grief and emotion will likely roll over you less frequently, but the pain of losing a spouse will probably continue for some time. Know that eventually you will feel better. Hang on to that hope.

Type of Death

The third common factor that affects the grief process is the type of death your spouse experienced. Do you think it is harder to lose a spouse through a sudden accident or through an extended illness? The answer may surprise you: Neither is easier. Death, no matter how it comes, is tough. Don't fall into the trap of trying to compare one form of death with another.

If you had some warning (such as a terminal illness), you may have had time to prepare. You may have been able to reconcile differences or address unresolved issues. Perhaps you had time to make funeral arrangements. Maybe you were able to prepare yourself mentally for the loss. But the research is contradictory and unclear concerning the effects of knowing in advance about a death. Most data now support few, if any, long-term benefits of anticipatory grief.[2] Even when you know the death is coming, most of us still find death itself almost unimaginable. That makes it impossible to prepare yourself emotionally for the anticipated loss.

One of my colleagues made a comment shortly after Rick's death that disturbed me greatly. He believed that because I knew my husband's prognosis for a long time preceding his death, I would be reconciled to the loss more quickly. But that wasn't true. Even when Rick was terribly weak and I had to care for his physical needs daily, he was still there with me. I knew cognitively he would die, but I wasn't ready or willing to accept it emotionally. When Rick died, my grief was deep, and I needed to work on it very intentionally.

Sudden death definitely does not allow you to prepare, which may prolong the period of shock and disbelief. When death comes without warning, you may have left something unsaid or undone, or you may have had a little squabble or disagreement, which now lingers in your memory. This unsettled state between you and your spouse may present another layer to your grief process. Remember that disagreements are normal in relationships and are typically resolved in time. If your spouse had lived, you would have discussed the conflict and worked through it. Trust that the methods you used historically would have been implemented again given time.

If your spouse committed suicide, you definitely have additional components to deal with. There may well be feelings of guilt, regret, or anger that are of a different venue because the death might have been avoided. Not knowing what was going on inside your spouse's mind to warrant taking his or her life is difficult and affects the grieving process. Be sure to keep in mind that each of us is responsible for our own decisions, as was your spouse. (See also the section "Complicated Grief" in chapter 3.)

The point is that everyone must grieve regardless of the type of death a spouse experienced. While you may be able to prepare for death in some cases, the real story is that the death of a spouse is difficult to deal with no matter what the circumstances. Avoid assumptions or judgments about the degree of difficulty associated with a type of death. That is unhealthy and counterproductive.

The Pastor Says

But seek first his kingdom and his righteousness, and all these things will be given to you as well.

Matthew 6:33

Facing Death

Martha was angry with Jesus. Don't let that thought shock you, but a very good friend of Jesus was extremely put out with him. Martha and Mary's brother, Lazarus, had gotten sick. Knowing Jesus had divine power for healing, the sisters sent an urgent message for Jesus to come. Bethany, their hometown, was only about twelve miles from where Jesus was. If you don't know the entire story, take a few minutes to look it up in a Bible (John 11:1–45).

Jesus purposely refused to come when the sisters called. He actually waited three days before setting out for Bethany. When your loved one was ill or in great danger, didn't you expect close friends to come quickly when called? Jesus didn't. He waited. In the meantime, Lazarus died. He not only died, but they had already buried him by the time Jesus finally got there.

The sisters ran out to confront Jesus. (Read John 11:21 and 32 with some emotion.) No formal pleasantries here. The first words out of Martha's mouth were, "If you had been here, my brother would not have died." Jesus, if you had only listened to me—if you had only come when I called—this whole thing would not have happened.

When a spouse dies, one of the first issues many of us deal with is regret. If only . . . If only I had called the doctor sooner. If only he would have taken another way to work. If only she could have had access to that new form of chemotherapy sooner.

Or we deal with a sense of guilt—guilt of things said or left unsaid. We experience guilt over things we might have done or not done. We think things could have been different.

In these situations, we tend to replay the events prior to our spouse's death. We want to do them over—do them differently. Maybe, just maybe, the outcome would be different. Or at least we might be able to have a different attitude toward them.

Understanding Death

We stand face-to-face with one of the greatest mysteries of Scripture—the mystery of death and life. Jesus used the illness and subsequent death of Lazarus to teach Mary, Martha, and the rest of us some basic facts about death.

First, in the matter of life and death, God sets his own time schedule. As strange as Jesus' actions might be to us, his delay in coming to the sisters was deliberate. He intentionally waited, knowing Lazarus would die. Jesus wanted them to know that death was not really such an overwhelming matter for him, which is why he referred to Lazarus as being "asleep" (John 11:11). But the disciples took him too literally, thinking that Jesus was denying the death of Lazarus. So Jesus finally had to say it directly, "Lazarus is dead" (John 11:14). In essence Jesus was saying that death, in the eyes of God, is no different than sleep. Just as easily as a parent can wake a child in the morning after a refreshing night of sleep, so easily can God resurrect those who have fallen asleep in him. Don't try to control the timing of death; you won't be able to. This is on God's schedule.

Another fact about death is that it always leaves an unfinished agenda. It is only conjecture, but perhaps Mary and Martha had things they still wanted to say to Lazarus. Especially in the case of sudden death, you have little or no time to say good-bye, little or no time to ask forgiveness for the offenses incurred between the two of you, little or no time to put to rest the dreams and visions that had shaped your future. So death is painful.

We mentioned in chapter 1 that Jesus wept at the tomb of Lazarus. This weeping was a recognition that death doesn't just affect those who die. Death invades life; it severs relationships; it stops life midstream.

Even children feel the pain of death. Eight-year-old Daniel wrote:

> Dear God. Here's a poem.
> I love you
> Because you give
> Us what we need to live.
> But I wish you
> Would tell me why
> You made it so
> We have to die.[3]

Don't miss the point of the Lazarus story. Death is not the final word; the end of the story is resurrection. For Lazarus, this resurrection was immediate. Jesus probably did this because he was only a few days away from his own death. He wanted his friends to have etched into their minds the power of God over death. He wanted them to know that the resurrection was real.

For us, however, the resurrection is somewhere in the future—perhaps the distant future. God sets his own schedule for life and death. Just remember for now that Jesus was telling Mary and Martha—and the rest of us—that death is not the final word.

Moving from the Grave to Grace

The death of a spouse throws uncertainty into our lives. Dreams and plans for the future are smashed; friendships often change; our view of ourself is significantly altered. We often wonder if anything remains in this world on which we can rely. In *My Utmost for His Highest,* Oswald Chambers reflects on the topic of "gracious uncertainty":

Our inclination is to be so precise—trying always to
forecast accurately what will happen next—that we
look upon uncertainty as a bad thing. . . . The nature
of the spiritual life is that we are certain in our uncertainty. . . . The spiritual life is the life of a child. We
are not uncertain of God, just uncertain of what He is
going to do next. . . . Leave everything to Him and it
will be gloriously and graciously uncertain how He will
come in—but you can be certain that He will come.
Remain faithful to Him.[4]

Our uncertainty is often fueled by our desire or need
to control the various aspects of our life. We worry about
a multitude of things. But Jesus' words from the Sermon on the Mount encourage us to move from the uncertainty of faith to a simplicity of faith. He says in
Matthew 6:33: "Seek first his kingdom and his righteousness, and all these things will be given to you as
well." Christian simplicity is a virtue. "Simplicity,"
writes Richard Foster, "slips in unawares. A new sense
of wonder, concentration, even profundity steals into
our personality. . . . Simplicity is a grace."[5]

Christian simplicity requires at least three types of
adjustment. First is a spiritual adjustment: "Seek first
his kingdom and his righteousness." I must lose my life
in order to find it. My life is gone. As deeply devoted
as I am to Christ, the death of my spouse means that
my way of life as I had defined it is gone. I have to begin
again. This is an act of grace, I judge—one not well
taken, and not one desired. But now I do have to ask
very pointedly and profoundly, "Well, Lord, what is it
that you want from me?" Should we not all ask that
question regularly? It is a simple question, yet one that
is wholly profound and complex.

A commitment to simplicity as defined by Matthew
6:33 also requires a mental adjustment. Christ not only

said, "seek first his kingdom and his righteousness," but
he assures us that all the rest will fall into place. This
may be hard to believe when your spouse has died. Paul
commands us to have no anxiety about anything (Phil.
4:6). Take control of your mind and your life. Take control of your attitudes, which are, for the most part, connected with prayer. Foster says there is an "intrinsic relationship between simplicity and prayer, especially
with that central aspect of prayer which is trust." Foster then tells this story:

> My children love pancakes, so once in a while I get up
> early to fix them a batch. It is interesting to watch those
> boys. They wolf down pancakes as if there were an end-
> less supply. They are not worried one whit about the
> price of eggs or my ability to provide them with pan-
> cakes. Not once have I seen them slipping some into
> their pocket thinking, "I don't know about Dad; I had
> better put away a little stash so that I can be sure of
> pancakes tomorrow." As far as they are concerned, the
> reservoir of pancakes is infinite. All they need to do is
> ask and, if it is in their best interest, they know they
> will receive. They live in trust.[6]

This leads to the final adjustment: Uncomplicate
your life. The more you possess, the more you will be
possessed by material things. The death of a spouse has
a way of cutting through materialism. Things just don't
count for much anymore.

After my spouse died, I started an inventory. I didn't
complete it. I quit counting because I was too embarrassed: two automobiles, a truck, three computers, four
television sets. I realized that none of these were really
worth anything. I looked at the world and realized how
right Foster was when he pointed out that those who
live in Western society ought not to pray that the rest

of the world come up to our standard of living. If they do that, we will exhaust the world's natural resources within ten years.[7] We ought to pray instead that we can modify our standard of living to match the seeking of God's kingdom.

My focus is no longer on earthly things. This lesson in simplicity began a movement from the grave to grace. In my human weakness, my eyes turned toward heaven where my late wife is. She was part of me, and in my grief, my desire to see her was so intense that I wanted to rid myself of all the things of this earth so I could be in heaven with her. But that was my human spirit speaking.

Simplicity says, My eyes are now turned to heaven because Christ is there. He is part of me, and my desire to see him is so overwhelming that I want to shed everything that holds me back so I can be in heaven with him. But I'm not in heaven. I'm on this earth—grieving.

Does faith really help in the grieving process? Yes and no. Don't let that answer surprise you. Faith cannot do certain things for those in grief. Faith will not insulate you from the pain of grief. Faith will not prevent feelings of anger, regret, or loneliness. Faith will not lift you above this process or excuse you from the tasks at hand.

Faith in Christ, however, will give you two essential things: the strength to endure and hope. Christ gives you the power to face death and take the onslaught of this last enemy full in the face. The death of a spouse hurts deeply, but Christ gives power to handle the hurt.

Faith also gives hope. "We do not . . . grieve as others do who have no hope" (1 Thess. 4:13 RSV). Jesus called Lazarus out of the grave in order to provide his disciples with a sure and certain sign that he himself would also come back to life. Faith assures you that grief will end; new life can come. Ultimately, of course,

Christ offers new life when he comes to create his new kingdom. But he also offers new life in the meantime—between the death of your spouse and Christ's return. The gospel is simple: "Seek first his kingdom and his righteousness, and all these things will be added to you as well" (Matt. 6:33).

3

What Is the Grief Process?
The Journey Itself

Mike had just come outside to check his mailbox when I came walking by. Mike's wife had died nearly a year earlier, and I hadn't seen him for about three months. The day was somewhat mild for a Michigan autumn with the leaves turning color. The air still had a hint of warmth in it. As we chatted, I quickly detected a new energy I hadn't seen before. Yes, he was doing pretty well. No, he hadn't thought of selling his house yet. Yes, the kids had been very helpful, but they have their own lives to tend to as well.

Then Mike said, "You know, Bob, I've been thinking I'd maybe like to start socializing a little bit. I never really thought I would ever say that. I loved Pat so very much. But I guess I have really come to realize that she is dead, and I am not. I think I really have to start working on rebuilding my life again."

Notice the movement in this story. Time passes, and attitudes change. What may have been totally inconceivable earlier is now becoming a possibility. Healing is occurring.

In this chapter we will deal with the issues of time, progress, and what some have called the *phases* or *stages* of grieving. Actually, we prefer to look at the grieving process in terms of *tasks*.

The Psychologist Says

We either make ourselves miserable or we make ourselves strong. The amount of work is the same.

Don Juan, *Journey to Xhan*

Grief is like a long valley, a winding valley where any bend may reveal a totally new landscape.

C. S. Lewis, *A Grief Observed*

Themes and Expressions of Grief

Different theories abound concerning how people move through the various experiences and feelings associated with the grief process. Earlier theorists used language suggesting that those who grieve progress through definite and predictable stages. They thought grieving was like walking through carefully defined rooms, passing from one to the next. Later research, however, indicates that grieving is not so predictable. Almost any experience or feeling a widowed person has subsequent to the death of their spouse is within the norm.[1]

While common themes and features may exist, we suggest you simply look at the various tasks of grieving without necessarily forcing them into a predictable pattern or sequence. Remember just a few simple things: Each person mourns in a different way, so no one can predict how *you* will feel. Reactions to grief are not like recipes with specific ingredients and guaranteed results. Allow your feelings of grief to surface and deal with them. The one outcome we all seek is to heal and move on. You may think that is impossible for you right now, but keep in mind the popular saying by Lao Tzu that "a journey of 1,000 miles begins with a single step."[2] Trust your feelings and don't try to compare yourself to others, being especially careful not to measure your progress by some predetermined stages or phases.

Grief expresses itself in four primary ways: physical sensations, feelings, behaviors, and cognitions.

Physical sensations. Your body's physical response to the death of your spouse may manifest itself in symptoms of tightness in the chest or throat, heart palpitations, hollowness in the stomach, dryness in the mouth, or shortness of breath. You may experience interruptions in your sleeping and eating patterns. Remember that these are normal symptoms of grief in response to loss. Keep in mind that no two people have the same reactions to the death of a spouse, but there are similar themes. Grief is not an illness, so you need not be alarmed by these physical components unless they persist for a period of time causing a continual problem in handling the usual activities of daily living. If that is the case, you would be wise to consult with your physician regarding available options. In the meantime, try to take care of yourself by eating food regularly (even if only in small amounts) and resting your body when you feel tired. Your physical symptoms should gradually decrease as you begin to deal with your loss.

Feelings. Anxiety, fear, anger, guilt, loneliness, sadness, and depression often emerge during the grief process. They are frequently experienced in a wavelike fashion, where their intensity ebbs and flows. You may initially experience shock or numbness even if your spouse's death was predicted. This numbness is a normal protective response. Gradually, however, the numbness will dissipate. Anxiety and fear about one's own survival are not uncommon. Powerful or intense anger may be directed at God, medical personnel, other people, or circumstances. At times anger may be combined with guilt and turned inward. Self-blame and shame may come in the form of embarrassment, remorse, and regret. You may exhibit a number of symptoms similar to that of depression, which are associated with the expression of intense grief. Actual clinical depression may occur if these feelings are internalized and not dealt with. Feelings are important and need to be expressed, examined, and worked through over a period of time. Try not to dwell on the negative statements about yourself, since this only attacks your self-esteem. You are a valuable person. Keep reminding yourself of your significance and that you did not die when your spouse died.

Behaviors. Grieving people also exhibit a number of common behaviors including crying, preoccupation, absentmindedness, withdrawal from others, detachment from surroundings, decreasing involvement in activities, being unaware of time and/or place, and a general sense of apathy. You may dream about your deceased spouse or sense your spouse's presence with you. Some bereaved people experience forms of visual or auditory hallucinations—actually thinking they saw or heard their loved one. These reactions are all normal in the initial grieving process. Widowed persons often cling to treasured belongings or some articles of clothing of their deceased spouse. They may find an uncanny closeness and connectedness to their loved one by wearing or focusing on these visual reminders.

Cognitions. Grief also manifests itself through cognitive changes. Widowed people often find they are preoccupied with themselves and the death of their partner, and they are often disinterested in normal activities. They may want to stop the world. After all, a significant person just died; how can the world just keep going on? Often they find it hard to concentrate on normal tasks. They can be confused and really begin to think nothing is important or relevant anymore.

The bereaved's spiritual life may change. Some embrace God and their religious practices more tightly. Others may reject them all together because they feel abandoned by God. Though it may sound strange right now, don't fight these reactions. Many people who experience the death of a spouse also face a crisis in their faith. But most often, they are able to return to a revitalized faith. So if you are angry at God and want to push him away, at least know that God understands you and what you are going through. If, on the other hand, you are clinging tightly to your faith and are afraid of expressing anger at God, trust that God can tolerate that as well. Eventually you can resolve your spiritual battle and be at peace with yourself and God. Work on the grieving process; God will continue to take care of you.

Tasks of Grieving

As we said at the beginning of this chapter, viewing the grieving process as a series of tasks rather than as a set of stages or phases may be more helpful. Grieving people do experience some common tasks, which you will need to face in order to get to the other side of grief. William Worden, Theresa Rando, and others in the mental health field have identified some basic landmarks of grief work.[3] I have adapted them to include:

1. Recognizing and accepting the fact that your partner is dead and unable to return.
2. Allowing yourself to experience all the feelings related to your loss.
3. Finding a place for the memories of your deceased spouse in your head and heart that adequately honors what you had together but also makes room to move on with life.
4. Adjusting to life as a single person by deciding who you are as an individual without your partner.
5. Reinvesting in life according to your own desires and interests.

Does this sound overwhelming? No doubt. I remember when I first realized the depth of my grief and how much work I had ahead of me in order to move on. It sounded impossible, and I had very little motivation to tackle any of it. However, with time and work, movement did occur. My thoughts and feelings did not remain static. Slowly things began to take on new shapes and forms as I traveled through this grief process. The process works through a series of small victories and setbacks. Remember, one step at a time eventually gets us farther down the road. C. S. Lewis observed about his own grieving process: "There was no sudden, striking, and emotional transition. Like the warming of a room, or the coming of daylight, when you first notice them they have already been going on for some time."[4]

Myths

A lot of myths and stereotypes have been handed down from generation to generation on "how to do it right." The frightening reality is that truth and fiction are woven together into many of these stereotypes, and unraveling them is difficult. Certainly, the most accurate perspective on grieving comes from those who have worked through the grief process.

While speaking at a Widowed Persons Services meeting, I was surprised at the intensity of the reactions from those who were widowed to what other people expected of them. They were frustrated, irritated, and sometimes hurt by the unthinking comments and expectations. They felt totally misunderstood at a time when others should have been surrounding them with empathy and understanding. Widowed persons should not have to deal with ignorance or naivete at the time when they most need help and support.

Through my personal experience and clinical practice, I have identified the following list of unhealthy myths and erroneous beliefs. Remember, although many people believe them, these are myths. They are not true.

Myth 1: Grieving extends over a set period of time, moves through definable stages or phases, and should decrease after three months and be completed after the first year.

Myth 2: The sudden death of a spouse is far worse than a death as a result of a long-term illness. Being able to anticipate grief makes the grieving process easier.

Myth 3: The loss of a child is far worse than other losses.

Myth 4: You should keep yourself very busy; too much time alone isn't good. Move on and occupy yourself with your current life rather than focusing on the deceased.

Myth 5: Don't focus on the fact that your spouse is dead; don't talk about the loss or tell the story of the death. If you don't think about the loss, the feelings will go away. If you have to talk about your spouse, say only positive things to elevate the deceased to sainthood.

Myth 6: One never gets over the loss of a spouse, and you will always feel the pain. Happiness is over forever now that you are widowed.

Myth 7: All previous friendships will fade and eventually be lost.

Myth 8: Look and act happy even if you are feeling awful. Be sure to accept all social invitations even if you don't feel like it or eventually you will be left out. Keep doing all your same previous activities because this will honor your deceased spouse.

Myth 9: Wearing your wedding ring means you are grieving; if you take it off it, you are done grieving and are ready to date.

Myth 10: You are not a whole person now that your spouse has died; there is a hole that can never be filled.

Myth 11: To go places alone or be by yourself says something negative or inferior about you—the "I must be undesirable or inadequate" syndrome.

Myth 12: You will never be able to resolve old conflicts that remained with your deceased

spouse since you can no longer talk together.

Myth 13: To have fun or laugh while in the grieving process means that you didn't really
care much for your spouse.

Myth 14: After a spouse's death, you must continue
to carry out the same wishes that your
spouse had when alive.

Myth 15: Widowhood means being sexually frustrated and never being able to have physical release.

Myth 16: Having friends of the opposite sex when
widowed means you must be considering
dating those friends or be romantically
interested.

Myth 17: Being alone is so lonely; living by yourself
is less desirable than with a partner.

Myth 18: If you had a happy and fulfilling marriage
prior to widowhood, you will be less likely
to want to have another relationship or
remarriage.

Myth 19: Men more than women need to have better self-control and handle grief cognitively.

I can understand how a widowed person could be
angry and frustrated by these expectations. My hope is
that as you move to the other side of grief, you can even
begin to educate your family and friends about the
grieving process. Unfortunately, most people are not
likely to ever understand your grief fully until they have
experienced the death of their spouse.

What can you do personally with these myths? Simply acknowledge the large amount of misinformation
surrounding grieving and attempt to remain as unaf-

fected by those unhealthy expectations and myths as possible. In other words, experience what you are feeling in a genuine fashion rather than trying to fit into someone else's format. Recognize that those who have never been widowed barely have a clue to what the process is really like. Give yourself the freedom to be yourself while grieving.

Complicated Grief

You perhaps now realize the wide range of "normal" experiences associated with grief. Hopefully this knowledge will assure you that you are not going crazy or experiencing something abnormal.

However, some people fail to grieve for one reason or another. They fall into a category known as *complicated grief*. Complicated grief can arise from a number of factors including an ambivalent relationship (unexpressed hostility) with the deceased spouse; circumstances surrounding the loss such as when the loss is uncertain, unofficial (e.g., no body can be located), or socially unacceptable or negated (e.g., death from AIDS or suicide); a past history of complicated grief reactions; and personality characteristics that produce an inability to express feelings or to tolerate emotional distress.

How can you tell if you fall into this category of complicated grief? One of the primary criteria is the amount of time you spend in grief on a daily basis compared with how long your partner has been deceased. Grieving is a process designed to help you live and love again. As time goes by, grief should be less of a focus in your life, and eventually grief should come to an end. This process can be slowed down or complicated by depression, self-destructive behavior, or early radical lifestyle changes in which one drastically replaces a social group or activities. If these issues are not dealt with as soon as they occur, your grief process may be significantly prolonged. In most cases, grief will be resolved in one to three years after the death of your spouse. Subsequent to that, if you find yourself experiencing intense, fresh grief as though your spouse just died, if you develop unconfirmed physical symptoms similar to those of the deceased or a phobia about illness or death, or if you are unwilling to deal with material possessions belonging to the deceased, you need to seek an assessment from a counselor or therapist who specializes in grief work.

If your grief continues beyond a reasonable period of time and has become complicated by other factors, you have a number of options open to you. First, with the help of a professional counselor revive the memories you may have avoided earlier surrounding the death of your spouse. Second, get a physical exam to rule out any physiological causes. Third, begin working more intentionally on some of the assignments suggested in subsequent chapters of this book. To work on complicated grief, it is very important to seek professional help. You apparently have run into some roadblocks working through grief on your own, and you could benefit from an objective perspective to help you get through to a resolution. Don't be afraid to get professional help. Grieving is difficult work, and sometimes assistance is needed in order to become healthy again.

The Pastor Says

Even though I walk
  through the valley of the shadow of death,

I will fear no evil,
  for you are with me;
your rod and your staff,
  they comfort me.

Psalm 23:4

Entering the Valley

These words from Psalm 23 are among the most familiar in Scripture. We memorize them as children; we
sing them during worship. As we grow older, the words
become a source of comfort and assurance when family members die and are laid to rest. Frequently we think
of those who are dying or have died as the ones who
have passed through this valley. Actually, the psalmist
had something else in mind. He wasn't thinking about
people who were dying; he was thinking about people
who were surviving. They were walking through the
valley, surrounded by disease, death, and other obstacles. One possible reading of the phrase "the valley of
the shadow of death" is actually, "through the darkest
valley."

When your spouse dies, the lights go out. Your life
may become dark, forlorn, and dismal. I remember a
few years ago talking with students at the seminary
where I teach about the sudden, tragic murder of a man
we all knew. He had just left church, was walking to his
car, and was shot during an attempted holdup. Suddenly, three children had no father, a loving wife was
alone, and they entered the valley. Valleys are dark,
often foreboding places.

Entering the valley is often beyond our control. We
generally do not choose to go there. The cancer strikes.
The heart fails. A driver, deep under the influence of

alcohol, careens across the median of the highway. A loved one dies, and we enter the valley.

Psalm 23 makes very clear, however, that you never enter the valley alone. You probably know the opening words by heart: "The LORD is my shepherd, I shall not be in want" (v. 1). The day after your spouse died, those words may have seemed hollow. What do you mean, "I shall not be in want?" I want my wife back! I want my husband alive! I want this whole thing to end. This is just a bad dream.

But notice that before you get to verse 4, which refers to walking through the valley, the psalmist says of God:

> *He* makes me lie down in green pastures,
> *He* leads me beside quiet waters,
> *He* restores my soul.
> *He* guides me in the paths of righteousness.
>   Psalm 23:2–3 (italics added)

You get the picture? God is the Shepherd; he is leading the flock. You do not enter the valley alone. As the hills begin to press in and the light of the sun begins to dim, the hand of the Shepherd is there to comfort and guide.

The initial shock, anger, and disbelief will dissipate. You come to the point where you begin to look up to see who is there. You can count on the Shepherd. He not only walks with you, he is the one leading and guiding you.

As you enter the valley, ride the feelings of shock, anger, and disbelief. Don't deny your feelings; God is big enough for you to pummel his chest out of sheer frustration and fear. Some friends may tell you not to cry because your spouse is in a better place. They may say there is no need for tears because now the suffering is all over. Poppycock. You cry just as much for yourself as for your spouse. This is not your spouse's grief; this is your grief. You are the one entering the valley.

Enduring the Valley

Entering the valley is one thing. Enduring the valley is another. I remember as a child listening to *The Lone Ranger* on the radio. I would sit with my ear glued to the speaker of the old floor radio. "Don't sit so close, you'll ruin your ears," my dad would holler. But I was fascinated by this masked man who could right the wrongs of the Wild West and rescue the innocent victims of crime and deceit. I also learned about box canyons. Having been raised in the Midwest, I didn't realize that some canyons in the mountains are like rooms with only one door. You have to come out the same way you went in. When the bad guys went into a box canyon, the Lone Ranger had them stymied. There was no other way out, and the masked man would capture them.

The valley of the shadow of death is not a box canyon. As often as we might describe our grief as a hole or pit (pictures that assume you have to get out the same way you got in), the valley of death has an exit on the other side. The psalmist is quite clear that you pass through this valley. Not only do you pass through it, but the psalmist now repeats that in walking through it "I will fear no evil, for you are with me" (Ps. 23:4). I find this amazing. Jesus had to walk the road to his death alone. Everyone else abandoned him. The disciples slept; others fled; Peter denied him. Christ walked alone; no one could walk that road with him. And on the cross, because of the weight of our sin, even God the Father momentarily separated himself from Jesus, wrenching from him the cry, "My God, my God, why have you forsaken me?" (Matt. 27:46). God forsook Christ once so that we would never be forsaken by him. I shall never leave you or forsake you is Christ's promise. Christ also promised that "surely I am with you always, to the very end of the age" (Matt. 28:20).

So Christ walks with us through the valley. And he carries his rod and staff—shepherds' instruments designed for protection and guidance. The shepherd's staff would be used to gently draw back to the fold any sheep that went astray. The crook of the staff was just large enough to catch the back leg of a sheep. The shepherd's staff was like an extension of his arm. Spinning and twirling the staff as he walked along with the sheep, the shepherd could quickly correct an errant sheep with the slightest move of the staff.

Even in our grief, we sometimes need to feel the gentle discipline and guidance of the Shepherd. So many decisions need to be made with so little energy to make them. What will we do about a headstone? When will we clean the closets? Will my friends still be there when this is all over? The Shepherd's staff guides us as we endure the valley.

The shepherd also carried a rod—a clublike device that would be used to ward off predators. This shepherd's rod is a symbol of God's defense of his people. Even in this valley, nothing will harm you. Did not the apostle Paul proclaim: "I am convinced that neither death nor life, neither angels nor demons, neither the present nor the future, nor any powers, neither height nor depth, nor anything else in all creation, will be able to separate us from the love of God that is in Christ Jesus our Lord" (Rom. 8:38–39)? That is the shepherd's rod. Nothing can stand in the way of the Good Shepherd—not even the death of your spouse, not even the

dark days in the valley. He walks with you as you enter
the valley, and he guides as you endure the valley.

Exiting the Valley

The psalmist also assures you that you will exit the
valley. Don't overlook the word *through* in the phrase
"I walk through the valley" (Ps. 23:4). You are not
meant to stay in your grief and despair. Valleys do not
last forever. Valleys are created by the peaks of mountains. As you emerge from the valley, the grandeur of
the mountain peaks come into focus. So verses 5 and 6
of Psalm 23 give you a hint of the majesty that is yours
as you exit this valley. The banquet awaits you. The
table is spread laden with the finest of God's gracious
gifts. Enemies can't touch you. You have the promise
of eternal goodness and love. You will dwell securely in
the arms of God for the rest of your life.

People hug a lot during funerals. After my wife died,
a few of my close friends had the freedom and sense to
hug me from time to time. Men need to be hugged too.
We need to literally feel the arms of a caring person
holding us tightly. We want to be connected. This is
the eternal promise of God in Psalm 23. He will take
us up into his arms, and we will be embraced by his love
and held securely for the rest of our earthly journey.

People need courage to hug you. Some may act as if
death and grief are contagious. They push away, usually
out of fear of confronting their own death. But when
your cup begins to overflow, your experience may in fact
help them confront their own death. Even at the beginning of your grief, your experience may begin to minister to others in their need. The anointing of God's
peace and grace flows over your head. His mercy so fills
your cup that it flows over to others. The comfort you

receive through Christ begins to comfort others as well. You are strengthened together, and you begin to emerge into the sunlight on the other side of the valley.

I look back now over the past several years. Sometimes I really wonder how I made it through the pain. Then I realize that I did not make it through the pain at all. God did it. "The LORD is my shepherd, I shall not be in want. He makes me lie down in green pastures, he leads me beside quiet waters" (Ps. 23:1–2). I am back there again—in the meadows. Through Christ, I have endured the valley. That part of my life's journey is over.

I may have to walk through that valley again because I have many people in my life whom I love dearly, and facing death is never easy. But God has led me through the valley once; he will do it again. Now I know that whether I am entering, enduring, or exiting the valley of the shadow of death, I will fear no evil. I am confident that his goodness and love will follow me all the days of my life, and I will dwell in the house of the Lord forever.

4

How Can You Take Charge of Your Grief?

Making the Most of the Journey

So now what are you going to do?" How often have you heard that question? A friend whom you haven't seen for some time finally stops by. The conversation recaps all you have gone through following the death of your spouse. Usually a few months after the funeral, other people begin to ask, "Well, what are you going to do now?" Will you stay living where you are? Will you travel? Will you get a different job?

You might initially react negatively to those questions. After all, what can I do? My spouse died! I'm all alone. I'm a victim. I just have to sit here and take it.

In this chapter we address the myth that you are powerless and a victim of circumstances. That may be true initially. The good news is that you don't have to continue long term to feel powerless in handling the death of your spouse. You can come to the point where you can take charge of your grief. You can manage it, that is, you can choreograph the process of grief and do things *intentionally* to get through to the other side. We don't agree with the old saying "It just takes time." Grieving takes work, intentionality, and assertiveness on your part. In this chapter and the next, we will touch briefly on a number of issues you may face. With each one we suggest a number of things you can do to help address that issue. These suggestions are reminders that you, and you alone, can take charge of your grief in order to work toward wholeness and healing.

The Psychologist Says

Any adversity not learned from is an adversity wasted.

Anonymous

How can you grieve most effectively? How can you help yourself get to the other side of grief? We will make suggestions in this chapter of tasks or assignments to help you through some of the difficult periods of grieving. The purpose is to resolve grief completely. I strongly believe each of us can affect the outcome of our loss so that we can finally say we are over our grief. That doesn't mean we won't have fond memories or a special place in our hearts for our deceased spouses. In one sense, your life will never be the same again. Your life, however, can be good—even great—though it will be different from your earlier life. Like the end of one song and the beginning of another, your new life does not have to detract from the one just finished.

The prescription to tackle grief work may seem strange to you. But if you are going to grieve anyway, why not work as hard as possible to help yourself? We know grieving takes time and work, but you can decide how much work to put into grieving. An analogy might be that rather than respond like a boat without a motor, tossed to and fro by wind and waves, you should start the motor and guide your boat through the storm until you reach the shore. You will then be helping to facilitate your grief work and doing as much as possible to get to the other side of grief. My hope is that you will actively tackle the pain rather than avoid it.

As we address a number of issues that you may face as you work through your grief, we will also provide suggestions to help you. Remember that although the issues may appear to be somewhat progressive, they are not phases or stages. You are invited to use the suggestions whenever you face these issues.

HELPFUL SUGGESTIONS
1. Attend a grief workshop or support group.
2. Read a few good books on grief.[1]

Tackle Grieving

Journaling

Perhaps you have heard the word *journaling*. You may think that journaling is like keeping a diary—listing or reporting daily activities and events. While a journal may include such a record, journaling is much more a record of feelings, emotions, reactions, and other thoughts associated with your present state of mind.

One of the first benefits of journaling is that you actually take time for yourself. You are acknowledging that you are important enough to spend time on yourself. Your journal is like a gentle friend who understands you completely. Through journaling, you can better figure out where you are coming from, what is bothersome, and what you must do in order to feel better. Since your journal records your emotions at various points, you can use it to assess your progress from time to time. So use this as a method to unload, process thoughts, identify options, and gain insights into yourself.

Over time, you may discover that journaling specifically about your deceased spouse leads you to journal about other important matters. As you work through your grief, you will face many other issues such as the ones dealt with in these chapters. Journaling can help clarify your thoughts and feelings concerning a myriad of issues.

HELPFUL SUGGESTIONS

Begin journaling about your deceased spouse by responding to the following questions:

- What do I miss most about my spouse?
- What do I wish I had asked or said to my spouse?
- What do I wish I had done or not done?
- What do I wish my spouse had said or not said?
- What do I wish my spouse had done or not done?
- What did I value most about our relationship?
- What was hurtful or angering about our relationship?
- What special memories do I have of my spouse and what memories will I keep alive?

- What will I take with me as a part of my spouse and our relationship to cherish?
- What living situation is difficult to deal with now without my spouse?

Use these ideas as a springboard to work through other issues specific to you, your deceased spouse, your relationship together, or what you would want in the future.

Funeral Rituals and Memorial Services

By the time you read this book, you probably have conducted a funeral or memorial service for your deceased spouse. This ritual really initiates the process of grief work, and you can already begin to take charge at the time of the funeral. Such a service is an excellent time to collect all the memories of your departed spouse that you hold dear.

You may be tempted to avoid the funeral service or a graveside burial, but these serve a vital function as you begin to face the reality of your loss. Certainly it hurts, but the pain and sadness only underscore how meaningful this person was in your life. You may be tempted to use medications to numb the anxiety or depression, but drugs only provide temporary relief. You will need to eventually face the pain. Avoid medications if at all possible so you can experience the full force of your feelings. Oddly, experiencing the pain of grief head-on is extremely helpful in moving along the grieving process. Do whatever you can to push through the pain, confident that as you face the pain, it will begin to dissipate.

HELPFUL SUGGESTIONS

1. As soon as you feel ready, reread sympathy cards and other correspondence. Look up the Scripture references, and try to memorize helpful sayings, stories, and verses.
2. Take an inventory of other expressions of sympathy such as flowers, meals, and visits. Recall who supported you during the initial days of your grief, and keep up your end of those friendships if that seems congruent to you.
3. Listen to the funeral tape at least monthly. Allow yourself time alone to cry, quietly reflect, be angry, or get in touch with other feelings. You may have been so numb at the funeral that these feelings were masked or suppressed. Listen again to the funeral meditation and even outline it for future reference. Be open to both releasing your emotions and receiving additional comfort through listening to this tape.
4. Write down significant comforting statements made at the time of your spouse's death and funeral.
5. Write about your thoughts and feelings as you tackle all of the above.

Belongings of the Deceased

Early in the evening on the day of Rick's funeral, my daughter and I thought it would be practical to clean out the bedroom closets. So we launched into that activity, sorting through all my late husband's clothes. What a whirlwind. I at least had the presence of mind to keep the more significant things until I could decide what I wanted to do with them. I will admit that it was helpful not to have to look at Rick's things every time I opened the closet, but I think it would have been healthier for me to have been the one to make the decision at a later time about when I was ready to complete that task. The day of the funeral was too soon; I was still very numb and disoriented from everything that had happened the days before.

Sorting through your spouse's belongings within a few weeks after the funeral, however, is a healthy thing to do. This activity may be painful, but here is one concrete thing you can do to help you face the reality of your new life. Perhaps you can do this in stages—this is what I call the layering approach. First, remove the clothing from the more accessible places and put it toward the back of the closet or a storage room. Then begin discarding belongings that hold no emotional attachment and periodically evaluate what is left. Try to take care of the majority of clothing within three to six months after the funeral. Certainly finish it by the first anniversary of your spouse's death.

This process does not have to be all or nothing. Two years after Rick died, I finally donated his bathrobe to charity. I decided I no longer need it as a comfortable reminder of his presence. I have kept a few articles of clothing simply because I like them, but I no longer wear them for any emotional significance associated with my deceased husband.

HELPFUL SUGGESTIONS

1. Deal with your spouse's belongings as described above.

2. Decide what you want to keep as memories and put them in a special place, box, or container.

Time Away and Vacation Plans

Vacations can provide a wonderful break from routine pressures. When you are grieving, however, you should carefully examine your motivation to get away. Trying to get away as a means of avoiding or even denying what you are going through is not likely to be very helpful. On the other hand, if getting away will provide you some time for solitude and reflection on your new situation, then you may benefit from a vacation.

You are the best judge of how directly you can face the pain of your grief. My advice is to face your grief as soon and as directly as you can so you can get on with your life again. But you may not be able to do it all at once, and occasional weekends or short periods away during the first year may give you the break you need to reflect and balance your perspective. However, be careful not to run away from a difficult situation because you will need to eventually face those fears and pains. Getting away by yourself during the first six months or even the first year after your spouse's death may be a challenge. The experience could be frightening, especially if you have never done anything like that before. But getting away will give you a taste of what life will be like on your own and hopefully will demonstrate that you have the capacity to manage things by yourself. Facing the pain of your grief is like beginning an exercise program and eventually running a marathon. Begin gently, but keep in mind your ultimate goal to heal.

> **HELPFUL SUGGESTION**
>
> Go somewhere by yourself overnight or for a weekend where you have never gone before. Choose a place that looks appealing to *you*, experience it by yourself, and then journal about your experience.

Self-Esteem and Self-Care

Self-esteem is probably the most critical factor in determining your ability to be alone. When you feel comfortable with yourself, you are more likely to enjoy some solitude. How confident you felt about yourself prior to your spouse's death will impact how confident or independent you will be now. If you saw yourself as a capable individual within your marriage, able to still function independently, you are more likely to see yourself as a whole or complete individual even though you are widowed. On the other hand, if your identity was so closely knit to that of your partner that you viewed yourself as an appendage and needing your partner, you will most likely require more time to heal.

Everyone who experiences the death of a spouse must go through significant adjustments in the area of self-esteem. You will naturally question your value and worth. Much of that value came through the relationship with your spouse. When that relationship ends, some people feel their life is shattered, forever hopeless, and over. Remind yourself frequently that you still are valuable, no longer as a marital partner but certainly as a person. We are created in God's image, and that doesn't change when we are widowed.

I found myself needing validation from friends to know that even though Rick had died, they still loved and cared about me. I needed to be reassured Rick wasn't the only reason we had done things together. I was surprised how needy I felt and that I wanted (or needed) so much reassurance. Rick had always been good at affirming me as a person. After he died, I had to learn how to give myself more of that assurance through other means.

Did you do nice things for yourself prior to your spouse's death? Did you ever go by yourself to a favorite nature spot, restaurant, shop, or event just for the fun of it? When your spouse or family wanted to do one thing and you wanted another, did you remain an advocate for yourself? Did you arrive at decisions considering everyone's perspectives *including your own*, or were you the one who usually compromised too much? If you acted in ways that demonstrated you valued yourself enough to do nice things even when no one else benefited, you may not have as difficult a time following your partner's death.

Taking care of yourself is even more important now that your spouse has died. Grieving takes a major toll on emotional and physical energy. Make sure you help yourself by eating at least three meals a day, getting enough sleep, and exercising on a consistent basis. The rest of life will be a little easier to cope with if you are doing these basic things. You have not stopped being important. If you maintain a healthy balance of food, sleep, and exercise, you will be better equipped to focus your thoughts, which will make healthy decisions more likely. Grieving will still be difficult, but at least you will have helped yourself to handle all that you can.

Helpful Suggestions

1. Write a portrait of what you like and dislike about yourself, including your strengths

and weaknesses; imagine that you are describing yourself to someone you don't know.

2. Describe yourself the way you think your spouse viewed you. What did he or she like and dislike about you and your marriage?

3. Write a description of the dynamics of your marriage—what you liked doing with your partner, what you only did because your spouse wanted to, how you made decisions (how the power was divided), what you wish had developed more in the time you were married, and what your future may have been like together.

4. Draw a circle and divide it based on the percentage of time and energy you put into each role or significant part of your life including spouse, children, friends, extended family, work, church, organizations, activities, or interests. This will help you see how much you spent on your relationship with your spouse in contrast to other interests.

5. Sort through a list of interests and activities in which you and your spouse participated and rate them on a scale of zero to five based on the actual amount of interest you personally have for that activity compared to that of your spouse.

6. Consider eliminating those activities or interests you did mostly or only because of your spouse. You now have the freedom to pursue exactly what you want to do. Perhaps you never pursued your own interests simply because your spouse had no interest and/or refused to be involved.

7. Go to some places you have wanted to see or explore (i.e., nature trails, beaches, parks, restaurants, civic events).
8. Enroll in a community education class to learn a new skill or pursue a new interest.
9. Take time frequently for your personal needs (i.e., take long baths, get a massage or manicure, take time to help yourself relax, or exercise more).

Be Gentle and Congruent with Yourself

"Be gentle with yourself" may sound a bit strange to you. You can be gentle with a baby, a puppy, or someone else who needs special care. But remember, you are at a point in your life when you need special care, and who is better equipped than yourself to give that gentleness? Being gentle with yourself simply means allowing yourself to have the time and space to work on issues that are important to you.

People will have a lot of expectations of you. They may pressure you to do things you do not want to do. Being gentle means giving yourself permission to be right where you are. Others don't know better than you what is best for you. You may sometimes question your own ability to determine what would be healthy for you, but you can still do it better than others.

One good strategy is to learn to trust your feelings and inclinations. Ask yourself how you (not someone else) think and feel about a particular situation, and then act consistently with your thoughts and feelings. That is what being congruent means—keeping thoughts, feelings, and behaviors in alignment. For example, you may be invited to go out for dinner with another couple. You think you would have difficulty being with them alone and carrying on a conversation; you feel uncomfortable about the potential situation; and so your behavior or action is to decline the invitation. That is being congruent with yourself and serves to maintain your integrity. You may decide later that you are ready to handle the situation, but always strive to be congruent with your thoughts and feelings.

Doing things that are upsetting or uncomfortable can compromise your integrity. Don't act a part; trust your feelings. Rather than internalizing or suppressing your feelings, go with them—at least in the early stages of your grieving. Give yourself permission to say no. You can always initiate later by letting your friends know you are now ready to participate in the group occasionally.

Helpful Suggestions

1. Make a list of some upcoming social expectations people may have of you. Journal about your thoughts and how you feel about those expectations, and then decide on an appropriate response.

2. Write down two or three statements you can use to remind yourself that no one knows you as you do (e.g., "I need to trust my own thoughts and feelings"; "Few decisions in life are in cement"; "Be myself"). Repeat those statements several times a day, especially when you have to make decisions about your activities. This practice is known as positive self-talk.

Firsts

You will soon discover that nearly everything you do soon after the death of your spouse, you will do for the first time. You will have to eat your first meal alone, go to church alone for the first time, celebrate a child's birthday alone for the first time. Facing these firsts is very difficult. The death of your spouse is painful enough, but now you also face grieving your own aloneness.

Now you have to face this issue: How are you going to handle these firsts—especially the holidays, birthdays, and anniversaries? Do you want to begin a totally new tradition in celebrating these events, or do you want to keep celebrating them in the traditional way? Or can you find some way to combine the old with the new? Obviously, no one can tell you what will be the best for you. All three options have some value depending on where you are in the grieving process. Escaping the scene certainly is a form of avoidance and probably not a healthy way to deal with these events over the long run, but if you are feeling extremely fragile and not able to cope at the time, this may be a reasonable choice. On the other hand, doing things exactly the same way you always did them quickly reminds you that your spouse has died. This method is a head-on, blatant confrontation of the loss. Are you ready for that?

Combining some old patterns with some new provides you an opportunity to evaluate meaningful traditions while allowing you to take some first steps in beginning anew. Some of your traditions were important largely because they were the product of consensus and compromise. Now that you are single, those compromises are not necessarily valid. So now you have an opportunity to evaluate what you value about the past and how you can make future celebrations truly your own.

HELPFUL SUGGESTIONS

1. Write about what were the most and the least meaningful holiday traditions for you.
2. Differentiate between what you did primarily because of your spouse's wishes versus what you wanted. Decide which of these you want to continue doing.
3. Decide what new traditions or customs you may want to incorporate into your family holiday celebrations because they are consistent with your own personal desires.
4. Journal prior to the special day or holiday about your anticipations and fears, and explore options of how you might handle them effectively.
5. Tell yourself that being alive is reason enough to enjoy the holiday as much as you can.
6. Journal about positive ways you can handle the challenges of the holidays. Reinforce these positive activities and explore what you might choose to do differently the next time.

Promises and Expectations—Nothing Is Sacred

What to do about promises made to your dying spouse is a sensitive area. On the one hand, you want to honor and respect his or her wishes. But so often, time and circumstances have changed. You may now begin to see these things differently. Decisions are directly affected by many factors. As with decisions you may have made about the holidays, all the decisions you made together were probably some form of compromise. Not only that, but the decisions were made within a specific time period. But time has moved on. Even your spouse may have changed his or her mind on some of these things now that the circumstances have changed.

Your spouse undoubtedly valued and trusted your decisions. Give yourself the freedom to evaluate prior decisions and make new ones when appropriate. Have the confidence that you and your spouse shared many values. The decisions that you will continue to make will undoubtedly still reflect those values. Your life is going on, and you have to live with the new decisions. Give yourself the credit and power to make the best choices possible.

HELPFUL SUGGESTIONS

1. Identify the basic promises or policies you and your spouse had. Journal about which ones you still agree with and why. From which ones might you deviate and why?
2. Discuss dilemmas with a close friend who listens well in order to gain another perspective.
3. Identify and list your values and beliefs that you are now incorporating into your life choices.

Grief Work Doesn't Just Happen

"Just give yourself time" are fighting words for me. You likely sensed that one of the themes of this book is to take charge of your grieving process and manage it; time alone is not enough to bring healing and wholeness, but time certainly can be your ally.

In this book we suggest specific tasks and exercises that may help you face the pain of grief and move on from there. We have given a number of suggestions in this chapter that will help you gain insight into yourself and a new perspective on your changing life. Let me summarize just a few other suggestions that will help you move to the other side of grief.

HELPFUL SUGGESTIONS

1. Talk to and with yourself both silently and out loud. Earlier we described positive self-talk as the repetition of certain words, phrases, or sentences that remind you of what would be the most healthy thing to do. Examples of healthy self-talk include: "I have my own life to live." "I can make decisions for myself." "I do have the right to be happy again." In addition to self-talk, you may even consider actually talking to yourself. I know the jokes people make about talking out loud to yourself, but we are created to process things cognitively and verbally in order to reach conclusions. When your partner died, you may have lost your kindred spirit; the one person who knew you intimately is gone. You need to find some way to continue this processing without your spouse being actually present. You can talk to an especially close friend, but that person probably still won't have the same level of connectedness you had with your spouse. So take time to process issues with yourself—talk to yourself aloud to understand issues and work things through. Verbalizing your thoughts helps you articulate them more definitively.

2. Think about some of your fondest memories (e.g., honeymoon, parenting joys, first and last kiss) and ponder them. Allow yourself to luxuriate in the memory. Picture every detail. One of the healthiest accomplishments you can achieve is moving these memories into a safe but accessible place in your mind and heart. Find a quiet place of solitude and replay these favorite events. Journaling about this experience after you have done it may also be helpful.

3. Be creative about getting thoughts and feelings out about special memories or conflicts you may have had with your spouse. Write some poetry, draw a picture, make a quilt, make a memory book or album, or write short vignettes of your life with your deceased spouse including factual information as well as your descriptions. Review and organize slides or pictures to make a video for yourself and your children.

4. Write a letter to your deceased spouse at various times during the grieving process. Consider doing one shortly after the funeral telling your spouse how you feel about his or her death, what you are wondering about, and other things he or she may want to know. You may also choose to write a letter on holidays, birthdays, your wedding anniversary, or the anniversary of your spouse's death. These letters would be healthiest if they included everything you were thinking and feeling—both the struggles and the joys of your memories and experiences.

5. Write letters to people who were important to you during your spouse's illness and death. Let them know your thoughts and feelings, especially with regard to their involvement. Express both your appreciation and any discomfort you may have had. Pouring out your raw feelings, even if that may not seem acceptable, is healthier than trying to censor your expressions and forcing yourself to be polite. These letters do not necessarily have to be sent. Writing them may be sufficient for your purpose, or you may decide to send an edited version.

The Pastor Says

I can do everything through him who gives me strength.

Philippians 4:13

Who Is in Control?

Paul's short letter to the Philippian church was not designed, initially, as a handbook for those who are grieving. The context was a church beginning to endure persecution while their founding pastor (the apostle Paul) was under house arrest in Rome. Their situation, however, suggests a number of parallels to the grieving experience.

Let me highlight a few verses that form a backdrop to Paul's confidence as he encourages his brothers and sisters to persevere under increasing persecution:

I always pray with joy . . . , being confident of this, that
he who began a good work in you will carry it on to
completion until the day of Christ Jesus.

Philippians 1:4–6

For to me, to live is Christ and to die is gain. . . . I am
torn between the two: I desire to depart and be with
Christ, which is better by far; but it is more necessary
for you that I remain in the body.

Philippians 1:21–24

Your attitude should be the same as that of Christ Jesus:
Who, being in very nature God, did not consider equality with God something to be grasped, but made himself nothing.

Philippians 2:5–7

Continue to work out your salvation with fear and
trembling, for it is God who works in you to will and
to act according to his good purpose.

Philippians 2:12–13

I want to know Christ and the power of his resurrection and the fellowship of sharing in his sufferings, becoming like him in his death, and so, somehow, to at-
tain to the resurrection of the dead.

Philippians 3:10–11

Rejoice in the Lord always. I will say it again: Rejoice!
. . . Do not be anxious about anything, but in everything, by prayer and petition, with thanksgiving, present your requests to God. And the peace of God, which
transcends all understanding, will guard your hearts
and your minds in Christ Jesus.

Philippians 4:4–7

I have learned the secret of being content in any and
every situation. . . . I can do everything through him
who gives me strength.

Philippians 4:12–13

We've been encouraging you to take control of the grieving process. From a mental health perspective, this is solid advice. The Bible, however, presents a tricky balance in this matter of control. The grand theological debate is between God's sovereignty and our responsibility. Who is responsible for your healing? Can you do it, or will God do it?

I judge that to be a false question. Actually, God uses you; God works through you. But finding the balance between taking responsibility for yourself and trusting God that it will all work out is tricky. I had to face that early in my grieving.

I am amazed by Paul's assertion that "I have learned the secret of being content in any and every situation" (Phil. 4:12). Contentment is not a characteristic closely associated with my life. As a matter of fact, I judge that few of us are really content, especially when our life has been turned upside down because of the death of a spouse. This lack of contentment may be all the sharper because I am by birth a male. In our culture, certain expectations attend maleness. Men should be fairly strong, controlling, and self-reliant. In addition to that, I am a De Vries. This may not mean much to you, but the De Vries clan takes these attributes of maleness to the next degree. We were raised to be superbly achievement oriented and successful, yet giving, compassionate, and kind.

I am also, by calling, a pastor and have identified with Jesus in saying that he did not come "to be ministered unto, but to minister, and give his life a ransom for many" (Matt. 20:28 KJV). I don't know how often I tried literally to fulfill that mandate by giving my life in sacrificial service to others.

So I struggle with this matter of control. We reflected in chapter 1 on how God is ultimately in control. We have even seen God's control as the Good Shepherd guiding us through the valley. But what does that mean for us? Does that mean you and I should just sit by and wait for God to bail us out? I don't think so. The matter of working on grief is not an either/or proposition: Either God gets me through this, or I work on it. The Christian life is always characterized as a both/and situation. One of the amazing passages of Scripture is listed above: "Continue to work out your salvation with fear and trembling, for it is God who works in you to will and to act according to his good purpose" (Phil. 2:12–13). You have no choice here. You are not faced with either God doing it or you doing it. You both do it, knowing that as you exert your own energy, God is already at work within you guiding, sustaining, and directing.

Doing It through God

In grief work, then, you need to find ways to assert your own control while still recognizing that God is the one empowering you to face this challenge. What are some of the things you can do, based on the words of Paul in his short letter to the Philippians?

1. *Develop confidence in God.* Philippians 1:4–6 calls you to remember that God is not a quitter. God doesn't start something and then quit on you. We have introduced you to the idea of journaling your feelings, emotions, and reactions to the various issues you face in the grieving process. You can also keep a spiritual journal.

My father preceded my mother in death by ten years. During those intervening years, my widowed mother wrote out a number of her prayers. None of her children knew about this until after she died. As we were going through her things, we found a tattered spiral notebook. Within that book were the precious words of a dear saint of God struggling with this issue of con-

fidence. Why, Lord? How can I believe in your goodness when now I find myself in this situation? As the
months and years progressed, however, you could sense
that she began to have confidence again that God
would finish the good work he had begun.

Write out your prayers. Journal about your feelings,
emotions, and struggles with God. Try to make a list of
everything God has done for you up to this point. Remind yourself that he has done good things for you, and
he won't quit on you now.

2. *Develop some confidence in yourself.* Philippians
2:5–11 is filled with theological mystery. You stand face-
to-face with the mystery of God becoming human. You
stand face-to-face with how God himself, in the form
of Christ, could suffer and die. You stand face-to-face
with the mystery of the resurrection. But Paul meant
to use that passage for a much simpler reason. He meant
to encourage the Philippians, and us, to have confidence in ourselves. The entire section begins with the
admonition to have "this mind in you, which was also
in Christ Jesus" (Phil. 2:5 KJV). Somehow, what Jesus
Christ did should serve as a model for us.

This passage may cause some confusion about the
issue of self-esteem. Many pastors and believers read
these verses to suggest that humility means setting myself aside or giving up on my rights. I should be meek
and mild, not worrying about myself because, after all,
isn't that what Jesus did? The answer is "not quite."

Jesus never gave up his true identity. Jesus never
stopped being the second person of the Trinity. Jesus
never quit being who he truly was. His circumstances
changed dramatically. He moved all the way from
heaven to earth, and he took on our form, but he never
gave up his own essence. Think about that for a moment. If Jesus, in coming to earth, gave up being God,

then he would not have been able to do what he did. He could not have performed miracles. He would not have had the power to forgive sins. Most of all, he would not have been able to endure the cross. Precisely because he continued to be true God, he was able to do these things.

How does that affect you? Paul says to have "this mind in you, which was also in Christ Jesus." Know that your circumstances have changed. Know that you probably will have to go through experiences you never wanted to endure. But also remember that ultimately you are still you. You are still God's child. You still have the same gifts, abilities, interests, and passions you had before your spouse died. The death of your spouse did not change who you essentially are. You are a child of the King, and as his child you must take charge just as Christ took charge.

During your period of grieving, you do have the right to tell people what you would like to do or not do. You do have the right to simply say, "I want time to be alone." You do have the right to keep a few precious mementos for a while. You also have the right to decide when to get rid of your spouse's belongings.

In fact, you likely need extra time now to discover who you really are. Having been married for a number of years, you need time (usually alone) to find out what being single really means. You may find that a spiritual retreat will be helpful. You can either go alone or find a spiritual retreat house staffed by trained spiritual directors who will help you walk through your spiritual journey.

Ultimately, however, you have to rekindle confidence in yourself. Know that ultimately your identity and your self-esteem is determined by one fundamental relationship—your relationship to God as his child.

3. *Develop confidence in the future*. The Scripture passages listed earlier are all based on the assumption that you have a secure future. Paul, old and in prison, was really torn between his desire to die and his sense of obligation to stay in order to continue his ministry.

Toward the end of her life, Char wanted to die. She was tired of the struggle to live and the pain was getting to be too much. She was torn, however, because another part of her wanted to stay. She wanted to be there when her children got married and when the first grandchild was born. But she knew, finally, that we all die. Her time had come.

Paul talks about joy in the face of suffering, triumph in the face of death, and peace in the face of trials. But this all rests on what he calls "the peace of God" (Phil. 4:7). This is a peace that goes beyond our understanding. But it is also peace you can experience fully so that, finally, you can say with Paul, "I have learned to be content" (see Phil. 4:12).

You can be content again. You can find that peace. God promises that can happen, but he also says you have to work for it. You have to take charge of your life. You have to work out your own salvation (Phil. 2:12), or in this case, you have to work out your own grief. You do this, however, knowing that God is at work in you to act according to his good purpose. As you move forward in your grief process, cling to the final promise of Paul in this letter to the Philippians: "And my God will meet all your needs according to his glorious riches in Christ Jesus" (Phil. 4:19).

5

How Can You Proceed in Your Grief?

Facing Obstacles on the Journey

Wee believe that a grieving person best addresses grief by realizing that as the days and months pass, the survivor must increasingly take charge of his or her life, directly address a number of issues or tasks, and design a process that will lead to health and wholeness once again. We firmly believe that grief is a process that has an end. You do not have to continue to grieve for the rest of your life. People who say that you never get over it misrepresent what is truly possible. Of course, you will never lose the precious memories; you will never forget the months and years that you had with your spouse. But the myth that you can never be happy again, that you can never function as a whole, healthy person must be directly challenged. Even those who have not experienced the death of a spouse often need to begin again. They may face a change in career, children growing up and leaving home as adults, or a move to another location. These are all examples of having to start over. As a survivor, you must also start over.

In chapter 4 we began a discussion of some of the basic issues associated with the grief process, and we will continue that discussion here. The issues in these two chapters have a slight chronological order to them, but we do not mean to imply that they represent phases you go through. Rather, the issues are somewhat chronologically conditioned. Some may persist longer through the grieving process, like the issue of loneliness. Others may present themselves only at certain times or when you are getting down the road toward healing.

The Psychologist Says

The capacity to be alone thus becomes linked with self-discovery and self-realization; with becoming aware of one's deepest needs, feelings and impulses.

Anthony Storr, *Solitude: A Return to Self*

Loneliness

Do you feel all alone? Do you think no one else knows or cares about what is happening to you? I remember a time about five or six months after my spouse died when I felt I could die and no one would even know for days or much less care. I had a deep, empty feeling. The reality hurts that no one on earth cares as intensely about you and what happens to you as did your deceased spouse. I experienced a feeling of total isolation wedded with deep pain, despair, and hopelessness.

There is definitely a feeling of loneliness in the face of death, with the reality that basically each of us is responsible for facing our own death alone. You may have helped support your partner through the process of dying—he or she had you as a kindred spirit during that difficult time. Now, as a widowed person, you face the frightening possibility that you will never have such a kindred spirit when your time comes to die.

About four months after Rick's death, I was at a basketball game and met a couple with whom my husband and I had socialized before his death. I was fine while I was at the game with them, but the reality of my loneliness hit me as I walked to my car alone, watched the other couple drive off together, and drove home without Rick. That was almost more than I could bear. I hardly saw the road through my tears as I drove home alone.

Then one day, still gripped by this misery and loneliness, I took a walk in my favorite woods near my house. I found myself reaching to God for his help, pleading that he would remove this pain, and then I sensed a crystal-clear response. I was not struck by a bolt of lightning, but I began to realize that God had given me the tools to help myself. I had to take charge of my life if I wanted to feel better. I had to realize that no one else was going to do it for me—I had to do it myself. I turned the corner and embarked on a new road of healing. Rather than merely reacting to other people and circumstances, I began to take the initiative. I did just a few things at first, but with each initiative, I felt better and stronger. I was taking control over some of the things I felt I could manage.

Loneliness is a terrible feeling. Don't mistake loneliness for merely being alone—there is a big difference. I can be alone and not be lonely. In fact, sometimes I find being alone very refreshing. But many people have been raised to think that being alone is detestable. From both a mental health and Christian perspective, though, solitude is a healthy thing. People who like themselves can be by themselves and enjoy that time without feeling inadequate or incomplete. A critical factor for enjoying time alone is having people in your life who care about you. Their support and connectedness balance out the alone time.

On the other hand, sometimes you may be surrounded by people and still experience loneliness. You may be experiencing that right now, because very few other people know how you feel or understand what you have experienced. Grief is not only a road you travel alone, it is also a lonely road. Know that lonely feelings are normal and that they will dissipate over time, especially if you begin to take the initiative to learn to be comfortable with yourself alone.

Actually we are talking about two different forms of loneliness: self-imposed and situational. Self-imposed loneliness is the deliberate act of separating yourself from others. Those who are widowed often do this for sheer self-protection. You may be invited to a wedding or a party that you and your spouse would naturally have attended, but you don't want to go now because you can't face going by yourself. But because you don't go, you feel left out. I should make it clear that this decision to separate yourself can be a healthy choice. This can be a form of taking charge of your life and deciding not to continue old patterns from your married life. On the other hand, separating yourself can become unhealthy if you use it as a form of denial or avoidance. Life goes on; you did not die. You have a new phase of life to explore and a myriad of personal needs to meet.

Situational loneliness is the type of loneliness that is inevitable after a death. Whatever companionship or kinship your spouse provided is no longer available. No one is around any longer to care about the "little things" after a day at work such as the harsh words you may have had with a coworker, the flat tire you had driving home, the compliment you finally received from your boss, or the squabble you had with your child that morning. Your spouse wanted to hear about those things, to share those moments. Now no one is there. You have lost a kindred spirit. That is why a death can be traumatic even after a long-term, debilitating illness. Your kindred spirit is gone. The person you shared with intimately, emotionally, and sexually is no longer there for you. Your roles are automatically changed, as well as your marital status, which does in fact affect your social group. You will need time to process this loss. There is no way around the fact that for many relationship-oriented people who want a special closeness with one person, situational loneliness will occur at times. At those times, you may think there is little you can do to relieve the loneliness. The healthiest option is to allow yourself to experience the pain and then plan some activity that will reconnect you with people.

Remember that loneliness is a perfectly normal response for two primary reasons: a lack of attachment to an intimate partner and a lack of community that comes through friendships. Perhaps you will decide not to reattach to an intimate partner later in your life. While grieving, however, it is not uncommon to think that this will never happen again or that you wouldn't want it to because you can't bear the heartache again. Just keep in mind that grieving is not an appropriate time to consider these options realistically. Whether you eventually choose to have another partner, you still have the option of maintaining and developing other friendships to meet your social needs. Making new friends is a healthy place to start when you are ready to reverse your self-imposed loneliness. Eventually, you will be able to accommodate the loss to some extent by filling in the gaps with healthy self-care, self-talk, and other friendships. Some widowed persons do, in fact, find another person down the road with whom they can develop another intimate relationship.

HELPFUL SUGGESTIONS

1. Analyze your feelings of loneliness. Try to determine the amount that is situational versus that which is self-imposed. For the portion that is situational, write about your feelings, expressing them honestly in whatever form they take. For the loneliness that is self-imposed, evaluate how much is helpful self-protection and how much may now be avoidance.
2. Learn to appreciate time alone by spending some time each day doing something that you enjoy by yourself. Learn to be a companion to yourself. Even begin to talk to yourself, and learn to reflect on your feelings.

Family Relationships and Friends

Remember the old saying, "Friends may come and go, but your family sticks with you forever"? The saying may be true, but the death of a spouse tests the loyalty of both family and friends. The death of a spouse is something like taking one piece off a mobile—all the other pieces have to adjust in order to keep balance.

Close relatives are often good people with whom to talk about reactions and feelings, and they often survive some readjustments. A familiar pattern is that parents may feel the need to begin parenting their adult child who has been widowed. Initially this may appear to be helpful, but in the long run this reparenting can be dangerous, if not disastrous. The one who is widowed must adjust to independent living rather than regressing to a more dependent state. Guard against that if you are widowed and your parents tend to be overly protective.

I attended my first Widowed Persons Services meeting about three months after Rick died.[1] The topic was "Changing Friendships." Someone said that by the end of the first year, the majority of my friendships would change or have faded away. I felt sick to my stomach. I already felt so alone, and the prospect of losing my friends as well seemed too painful to bear. I put the comment out of my mind, dismissing it as untrue. But over the course of time, the nature of my friendships has changed. I still don't know exactly why this happened. Any number of reasons could account for it: Some may have been uncomfortable with the thought that Rick had died; some may have been uncomfortable relating as a couple to someone who was a single female; others perhaps were more connected to us as a couple through Rick than through myself. I still have many of these friendships, but they have been significantly restructured. After two years, my relationships with friends has indeed changed.

So you will have to decide how to take control of this aspect of your life as well. First, I encourage you to avoid any impulsive decisions. Allow yourself to respond to each individual friend and situation. Collect data over the first year of your bereavement. Then you can begin to make some decisions for yourself because you will be able to see your network of friends in a new light without the heaviness of intense grief clouding your perspective.

One unavoidable reality is that persons who are widowed should really expand their social horizons to include other people who are also single. Don't neglect your married friends, but couples tend to relate mostly to other couples and cannot meet many of the needs you now have as a single person. Other singles (either widowed or divorced) may have more things in common with you. Attend special support groups for those who are widowed, but in time expand your horizons to other clubs or activities that are more socially oriented.

Helpful Suggestions

1. List friendships you have valued. Assess the nature of those friendships and identify whose friends they were (mostly yours or your spouse's) and which of these friendships you think you would most like to keep.

2. When you have determined which former friendships you want to retain, honestly express your desire directly to them and make some suggestions on how the friendship can be maintained while still being fulfilling for you.

3. When you get to the point where you are beginning to take charge of your life again, identify some groups in your community that may offer you the prospect of developing new friends, especially with other single people (e.g., Widowed Persons Services, church singles groups, choir,

ski or bike clubs, community education classes).

4. Once you have met some single people you think could be your friends, initiate contact and begin to socialize together.

Meeting Your Sexual Needs

How you approach the issue of sexuality as a recently widowed person will depend largely on your background. The issue of sexuality for a single person is, indeed, very provocative. Even within Christian circles, people hold widely varying views as to what is permissible and/or healthy. As a Christian psychologist, I have had to face the issue regularly. While we do not have the space to go into a deeper discussion of sexuality, let me share with you these basic tenents that I hold as valid:

- Sexuality is part of God's creation. Each of us is created with varying levels of sexual desire. This sexual desire is as natural and good as any other appetite we may have.
- Sexual desire finds its healthiest expression in a married, partnered physical relationship that is mutually satisfying.
- It is unhealthy for single persons to engage in intimate physical contact merely for the release of sexual tension without a commitment to a long-term relationship.
- Self-pleasuring (masturbation) is an option available to single persons to help reduce the physiological sexual tension that develops as part of being human.

- Self-pleasuring to orgasm will give adequate physical release, although this activity fails to provide the emotional fulfillment that a close partnered relationship can provide.
- Self-pleasuring when married is an ineffective permanent or frequent option for sexual fulfillment. It is a way to modify sexual desire when a partnered relationship is not available (e.g., when one's partner is seriously ill or absent).

As a widowed person, your sexual desire will depend on many factors, such as the intensity of grieving, your innate sexual desire, the nature of your previous sexual experiences with your deceased spouse, and the degree to which sublimation (using sexual energy in nonsexual ways) can be used. Meeting your sexual needs without a partner is, without a doubt, one of the most difficult issues surviving spouses face, and it may add frustration and sadness to your loss. You will need to take charge and make some choices so you do not respond impulsively and in an unhealthy way to a potential sexual situation. You may choose to use self-pleasuring to effectively modify your sexual tension as a single person or in the interim while you seek to develop a new life and new relationships.

Helpful Suggestions

1. Learn to accept the fact that sexual urges are normal and healthy. Having such urges even when grieving is normal, and meeting those needs individually is natural and healthy.

> 2. Read books to help you understand your
> own sexuality and to enhance your com-
> fort level in meeting your sexual desires.[2]

Heterosexual Friendships, Dating, and Remarriage

I can still remember sitting on our porch overlooking the lake. Rick was saying that he wanted me to remarry after he died. I can still feel the nausea and repulsion I felt at his words. I begged him to drop the
subject, but he persisted, saying that he needed to talk
about it. He truly was a wise man.

Two years later I am sitting on the same porch writing this chapter. The idea no longer repulses me, and I
have the added benefit of knowing that Rick wanted
my life to begin again, even to get married again. He
knew how much I loved having our close, committed
relationship. He also knew I was the type of person who
would want that deep level of communion with another
person.

You probably have heard people say that if you truly
loved your late spouse you would somehow devalue that
marriage or be disloyal by marrying again. Do you know
that the reverse is really true? Research shows that a widowed person who had a happy and fulfilling marriage
the first time is more likely to desire another very satisfying relationship or marriage.[3] That really makes sense.
If we liked doing something once, wouldn't we want to
do it again? Doing it a second time in no way detracts
from the first. You are not trying to duplicate or replace
the first marriage. Rather, you are seizing another opportunity to develop a deep, caring relationship.

In order to make room for a new relationship, however, you must be able to convert your first marriage
from one of the present to a loving memory. It is also

necessary to see yourself as single and be grounded as an individual before moving into a new relationship. Making that conversion not only takes time, but you need to be very intentional about it.

Women face an especially discouraging situation simply because current statistics indicate that there is one single adult male for every four single women.[4] Even though a woman may eventually decide to remarry, her prospects may not be very encouraging. This may not be true for a man because he still has four times more women to choose from. However, he may not find a woman who meets the criteria he has set for another partner.

How does an adult go about meeting a potential partner? You may think you have to revert to old high school patterns. As an adult, the simplest advice is not to look for a partner but begin to develop friendships for their own sake. If that goes well, if you feel open and comfortable with a friend of the opposite sex, then begin to discuss up front whether both of you may want to move into a dating relationship. You cannot talk too much about relationship issues, including the pros and cons of dating (versus remaining friends), what each of you expect from dating, and the long-term objectives for the relationship. Don't wait until you get deeply involved to discover that one of you wanted the goal to be marriage while the other was looking for a long-term friendship. If you feel awkward or uncomfortable talking about these things, you are better off trying to work through those feelings than to block communication. Remember, no one has to remarry. Many widowed persons develop a number of cherished friendships with persons of both sexes as an alternative to remarriage. Remarriage is only healthy and significant if it enhances a person's life in a positive way.

HELPFUL SUGGESTIONS

1. Assess the nature of the friendships you have with singles of the opposite sex, including the ways they enhance your life. Look at which ones, if any, hold potential for a dating relationship.
2. Evaluate your own desire to remarry. List the pros and cons for yourself.
3. List the characteristics and criteria of a person you would seriously consider for dating and possible remarriage. Then make a list of those characteristics you want to avoid at all costs.
4. Evaluate realistically what you have learned about yourself and partnering from your previous marriage. What did you like? What would you want to have or do differently in a new relationship?

Facing Your Own Death

The death of a spouse has the potential to hurl you headlong into a confrontation with the possibility of your own death. As John Donne said, "Ask not for whom the bells toll; they toll for thee."[5] If you were present when your spouse died, you may have imagined how you might feel if you were the one actually dying. Maybe you have given more thought to your own wishes and desires should you contract a terminal illness. In the process of discussing funeral arrangements and cemetery plots, Rick and I worked through our beliefs and desires together. Had he not been diagnosed with a brain tumor and had we not had time to talk about these issues, I doubt we would have ever broached

the subject of death until we were well into our retirement years. I am grateful I was forced to deal with some
of those tough decisions. I find myself much less fear-
ful about my own death because I have already walked
the road with someone I dearly loved. Even though I,
of course, have not experienced that final phase of my
life, I am much more aware of what is involved—some
of the unknown has been made known. In addition, my
belief that death is only one short sleep away from eternal life with God comforts me.

Psychologists encourage people to face their fears and
deal with their anxieties in order to decrease or negate
the power of those fears. I endorse this process of confrontation, especially in facing your own potential fear
of death. Death is a certainty for all of us. You have an
opportunity to face it squarely now, thereby enhancing
the rest of your life. Quoting the Swiss national an-
them, Isak Dinesen wrote in *Out of Africa,* "He who is
prepared to die is free."

If your spouse's death was sudden, you also had to
deal with the reality of death as a fact of life. With an
unanticipated death, you were forced to face it in a more
traumatic manner. You had no quiet chats about death
as your spouse weakened. But regardless of your circumstances, you are in a position to develop a healthy
perspective about life's fragile nature and our ultimate
purpose here on earth.

HELPFUL SUGGESTIONS

1. Consider your thoughts and feelings about
   how you would deal with your own death.
   What arrangements would you want? Write
   down your wishes and explain them to a
   person you trust. Consider making prior
   arrangements through a funeral home.

2. Identify the meaning of life and death from your own spiritual perspective in order to form a framework to deal with the reality of dying when it is your turn.
3. Live your life to the fullest each moment of every day so that whenever your life ends, you can rejoice at how you have lived without any regrets.
4. Get your estate in order by arranging for a will, living trust, and durable power of attorney for health care so that your wishes will be honored.

The Pastor Says

I am the only one left.

1 Kings 19:10

God has said, "Never will I leave you; never will I forsake you."

Hebrews 13:5

Lonely, but Not Alone

Your experience may have been similar to mine. After the funeral, after the cemetery, after the social time, everyone goes home. Friends go to their families. Your brothers, sisters, cousins, and other relatives go back to their lives. Maybe someone stays with you for a day or two, but they finally leave. Even if you have children at home, the time comes when they go to their rooms and you have to climb into bed—alone. The sheets are cold; the room is empty. You hear noises you never heard before. Shadows dance in an eerie light.

You feel like a little kid again—alone and afraid. What once was a place of physical and emotional intimacy with your spouse is now a place of loneliness. No one is there to cuddle or hold you. The bed is cold.

Loneliness is perhaps the greatest and most universal experience of being widowed. Feelings of abandonment or a sense that you have actually lost an extension of your own body can overwhelm you. Some of the Psalms, especially the laments, give voice to those feelings.

> O my God, I cry out by day, but you do not answer.
>
> Psalm 22:2

> Hear my prayer, O LORD;
>   let my cry for help come to you.
> Do not hide your face from me
>   when I am in distress.
> Turn your ear to me;
>   when I call, answer me quickly.
>
> Psalm 102:1–2

God appears to be far from us at times like this. We truly wonder if he cares, if he sees, if he will do anything for us.

Travel back into the Old Testament. Elijah was one of the greatest prophets in the history of Israel. Imagine yourself as a spectator on Mount Carmel. (You can read the entire story for yourself in 1 Kings 18 and 19.) Wicked King Ahab and his even more wicked wife, Jezebel, had Israel in their grasp. Ahab and Elijah had come together on the top of the hill for the duel of the century. The battle was between Ahab's gods and Elijah's God. Whichever god could light the fire on the altar would be the winner. That god would end the drought that plagued the countryside and would have the loyalty of the people. Ahab's priests prayed, then ranted, raved, danced, and finally cut themselves trying to get the attention of their gods. Elijah mocked and jeered. He was feeling great—a type of Mohammed Ali of the Old Testament. "Hey, your gods must be sleeping! Shout a little louder," Elijah cried.

Then it was Elijah's turn. Before he began, he totally doused the altar with water—three times. Then a simple, quiet prayer. Suddenly a firestorm crackled from the heavens. The altar, the wood, the stones, the water, and the surrounding ground were all instantly cremated. Elijah won. The rains came, the people cheered, and all the prophets of Baal were put to death. Life couldn't get any better than this.

Prior to the death of your spouse, you may have felt just like that. Char and I did. Everything was going fine. We each had our careers. We had three wonderful children. Everything was in place, well ordered and well oiled.

But something weird happened to Elijah. After this great victory, something snapped. We find him running away, deeply depressed, sitting by a little creek wishing he would die. And what is the reason he gives for this turn of attitude? "I am the only one left," he cried (1 Kings 19:10, 14). For some reason, an overwhelming sense of loneliness threw Elijah into a deep depression. Even the best of victories, the highest achievement, was not enough to spare him from this agony.

The answer he received was simple: "You may be lonely, but you are not alone." Whisper those words to yourself. Write them down as a good script for self-talk: "I may be lonely, but I am not alone." Elijah was sent on a scavenger hunt to find God. God sent winds, earthquakes, and fire. God sent the spectacular events, but Elijah didn't find him there. God wasn't there in the way he was a few days before on Mount Carmel. Then God came to him in a "gentle whisper" (1 Kings 19:12).

You need to be quiet to hear God whispering. Being alone helps. Now is the time for no distractions, no competition for your attention. In your grief, focus quietly on yourself and God. For God was saying to Elijah very clearly, but quietly, "You are not alone. Don't think you are in this by yourself. I have over seven thousand faithful friends in Israel" (1 Kings 19:18).

You may be lonely, but you are not alone. Thousands of others have gone through similar experiences. Countless others also face the issue of being single again after having been married.

One Is a Whole Number

Let me return for a moment to a theme I began to develop in the previous chapter—the issue of self-esteem. Frequently, married couples begin to blend their lives so completely that their identities are woven together. When one person dies, the other is immediately thrown into a period of redefinition. Men may try to redefine themselves through their work. Women may try to do that through their friends, family, or parenting. We say to ourselves (implicitly) that we are what we do or we are what other people think we are. You now have to stand alone. You have to discover once again what it means to be an individual child of God.

Being a single adult is likely a scary prospect. We live in such a coupled society. Everyone assumes either that you are married or that you are not quite complete if you are not married. The apostle Paul, however, makes his position quite clear. You do not have to be married to be a complete person in the sight of God. In 1 Corinthians 7 Paul deals rather extensively with the matter of marriage. This passage usually isn't quoted at wedding ceremonies because, for one thing, it is quite complicated, and because Paul sees many advantages for remaining unmarried. Paul actually starts the chapter saying, "It is good for a man not to marry" (1 Cor. 7:1). He then discusses the pros and cons of marriage, concluding that an unmarried person can concentrate on "the Lord's affairs" better than a married person (1 Cor. 7:32–33). Whether you agree with him or not, the point is that the Bible does not command you to be married in order to be a whole and complete person.

Years ago, while pastoring a congregation near a college campus, a young woman asked me about the church's view of remaining single. She apparently was being pressured to find the right man. I wrote her a long letter dealing with that issue. Among other things, I wrote:

> As you very well realize, our personalities are determined and conditioned to a great degree by the fact that we are either a man or a woman. You can never divorce yourself from your sexual identity. This sexual nature is not limited merely to a possible relationship to a husband or wife. Everything you do is colored by an awareness of who you are sexually. What Paul is saying in 1 Corinthians 7 is that no matter what you do with regard to marriage, you can glorify God in your sexuality—in your womanhood or manhood. With regard to marriage, Paul's basic guideline is that everyone should lead the life God has given to them. Marriage is an option not a requirement. You can be a whole person either way. Marriage does not make you complete, anymore than being single makes you incomplete. Trust the Lord's leading. He will not fail you.

After having been married for twenty-eight years, I had to struggle with my singleness for a long time.

I needed to find the freedom to love myself. Certainly I could love someone else; I had already demonstrated that. Now the issue is: Can I love myself? Can I be kind to myself? Can I enjoy myself, not in some abstract way, but as a single man? These may also be important questions to ask yourself.

You are not alone. Read again that portion of the Sermon on the Mount recorded in Matthew 6:25–34. The point of the passage is that your heavenly Father knows what you need. In order to take comfort from that passage, however, you need to do one other thing. To truly be comforted by God in heaven, you need to close the gap between earth and heaven. The death of your spouse may be a step in that direction if you have confidence that your spouse's faith reserved for him or her a place in that home of many mansions (John 14:1–4). What about you? Are you ready to face your own death as well?

I was raised in a church tradition that used the Heidelberg Catechism as a teaching tool. The first question and answer of the catechism is beautiful in its simplicity. The question is: "What is your only comfort in life and in death?" And the answer is straightforward: "That I belong, body and soul, to my faithful Savior Jesus Christ." I belong, fundamentally, not to a husband or a wife nor to my children, my career, or this world. I belong to my faithful Savior. Do you long to see him? Have you faced the reality of your own death as you grieve the death of your spouse?

In this regard Paul reminds us that we do not grieve as those without hope (1 Thess. 4:13). He doesn't mean that we do not grieve. He doesn't want to suggest that our pain is less or our task simple. But he is reminding us that we have a hope—a hope in the resurrection when we will all stand in celebration before the throne. The time will come when Jesus Christ (the groom) will come prepared for us, his church (the bride). And a loud voice will declare:

Now the dwelling of God is with [humankind], and he will live with them. They will be his people, and God himself will be with them and be their God. He will wipe every tear from their eyes. There will be no more death or mourning or crying or pain, for the old order of things has passed away.

Revelation 21:3–4

The new world is coming. Now is the time to find your place in it.

6

How Does Gender Affect Your Grief?

Being Yourself on the Journey

It is good to have an end to journey towards;
but it is the journey that matters in the end.

Ursula K. LeGuin

Society has a profound effect on shaping our attitudes and behaviors about gender. The feminist movement has only served to highlight the differences and similarities of gender.

Most of our behaviors as men or women are learned from our parents and other significant people when we are growing up. We are taught to "be a man" or "act more ladylike." Men are typically praised for being thinkers, being in control, and being competitive and successful. Women, on the other hand, are conditioned to be relationship-oriented, feeling-based, sensitive, and caregivers. Boys play with soldiers, trucks, and guns. Girls play with dolls, lipstick, and old dresses.

In recent years these traditional gender roles have begun to change. We are beginning to recognize that men and women share many common traits and that each gender is enhanced as they develop the traits often associated with the opposite sex. Men can be caring. Women can be competitive and successful. In neither case do these characteristics violate their gender identity.

Most of us, however, still function with more traditional gender expectations and roles. How we view ourselves as a woman or as a man has a profound effect on how we manage the grief process. How can you be yourself on this grief journey?

We want to accomplish two things in this chapter. First, we will describe what seems to be the conventional wisdom about the impact of gender on the grief process. Then each of us will tell our personal story of how we managed the grief process, particularly as a man and a woman. We invite you to reflect on your own story as we tell our stories of:

- how the loss was experienced
- how the loss was expressed
- how the loss was related to our work or career
- how others reacted to the loss
- how we viewed the issues of sex and remarriage as we proceeded through the grief process

How the Loss of a Spouse Is Experienced

Both women and men experience much pain and sadness and express a deep yearning for their deceased spouse. Both genders basically experience many of the same feelings, emotions, and challenges. However, there are definitely gender differences in the grieving process.

Many men, for example, describe their initial experience following the death of their wife as losing a part of themselves, as if they had been dismembered. "It's like losing an arm, or a leg—no, actually much more than that—like losing a piece of myself" is a common male response.

Women, on the other hand, generally talk of abandonment, of being left alone. "I feel so lonely—so isolated. I'm all by myself, and I just can't stand it" is a common female response. She had counted on her husband to provide her with protection and a sense of well-being. Those are now gone.

These reactions are likely caused by the way in which society has defined traditional male and female roles. Typically a man constructs an integrated system for his life, consisting of work, marriage, family, and leisure. When his wife dies, a part of that connected system is missing. She was a necessary part of his total system that allowed him to function because his marriage and his work were both in the same sphere. Hence, he feels as if he has lost a part of himself. He has been dismembered; part of his system has been cut off. This is likely one of the primary reasons a man may tend to remarry much more quickly than a woman—he wants to refill the hole in his total system.

A woman, on the other hand, tends to develop marriage and career in relatively disconnected or individual spheres. Females alternate between marriage and work and keep them more separate than do men. A woman who has followed the traditional model of being a helper to her husband, finding her identity more in family and marriage relationships than in a career or other social relationships, experiences her husband's death as more than a loss—she has really been left behind. The central hub of the all-important sphere of marriage and family is now gone. She is left alone.

We want to reinforce that these are traditional gender roles; they are conventional wisdom. You may be an exception or have experienced a significant variation on these themes. We certainly have.

Susan's Story

Six years of marriage—it is hard to describe the depth of our happiness! Our daughter was born; we were both well established in our careers; we had a new home; our lives were filled with peace and contentment. Rick and I had it good.

Then suddenly a grand mal seizure struck without warning. A week later, Rick was diagnosed with a brain tumor. Our daughter, Sarah, was just eighteen months old at the time. The popular song "We Almost Had It All" captured our feelings. We did almost have it all—except for an ugly pathology report; except for a malignancy that would affect our lives for the next seventeen years.

We struggled with the question, Why, God—why us, when we had so much potential to do so much good for others? We resolved to stand on our faith and be used by God in whatever course our lives would take. As the next seventeen years unfolded, we experienced all sorts of ups and downs, good times and bad. But through it all, God's grace was evident. We lived life to the fullest, even after Rick's frontal lobe was removed at the Mayo Clinic seven years prior to his death. Rick had phenomenal faith. It got him through his hell on earth in the healthiest way he could manage. Rick died on October 18, 1994, at the age of forty-seven. He is at peace now, and I am at peace for him. I don't wish him back here now; he suffered enough.

The last seven years of Rick's life were spent as an invalid. He had to give up his profession, and during the last two or three months of his life, he couldn't walk. He needed a lot of physical care. Family, friends, and hospice provided invaluable support.

When Rick died, I was exhausted. While he was alive, I had determined to do and be all that I could, so I pushed myself to be a good spouse and caregiver while I also continued my full-time clinical psychology practice. I functioned on two to four hours of sleep a night for several weeks prior to his death, but I made myself hold it all together, even during the visitation and funeral. I did it for Rick; I did it for Sarah; I did it for myself.

Rick and I had talked for endless hours during the summer prior to his death. We talked about how he felt about life. We talked about his pride in and hopes for our daughter, Sarah. We talked about how he wanted to die and what the funeral would be like. I wanted to honor his wishes and handle myself in the most noble way, so I took charge of things. That helped cover my feelings so I wouldn't break down at times I thought inappropriate, but I fell apart when no one was around. I didn't want to do life by myself. I wanted my life's mate back. It wasn't my idea to be widowed at this young age. I wanted to grow old with Rick.

Beginning about the fifth month after Rick died, I was so down I wanted to kill myself. I knew I wouldn't do it. My Christian faith was solid—but that didn't prevent the feelings of despair that lasted for a few months. I was so miserable. I had never felt so alone and deserted in all my life. Rick was my kindred spirit, the person with whom I shared everything. Now there was no one—just a huge hole.

Our daughter had begun her freshman year at a university in Pennsylvania, so I was not only adjusting to

Rick's death but also dealing with empty-nest syndrome.
My daughter was becoming an adult and didn't need me
either. She was quite responsible and independent, and
she was developing her own life. That was healthy, but
I felt empty. I felt emotionally drained most of the time.
Going to bed alone at night was so hard that I prayed
God would just let me die and take me to be with Rick.
I wanted out of this life. It took me a long time to real-
ize that I indeed had not died; my life wasn't over. My
life still had meaning and purpose, but I had to find it.
My life could be filled again.

In the meantime, I didn't know how to get beyond
the pain—the grief hurt something fierce. I had always
told clients that a cardinal sign of resolved or completed
grieving was when there were no more emotions to let
out. My emotions felt like a bottomless pit.

My emotions were closely associated with a number
of firsts—especially during the first six months. These
firsts began the day after Rick died. It was his birthday.
Thanksgiving and Christmas followed shortly after that;
then there was Easter. Everything that is significant to
you in your life, such as a holiday or birthday or anniversary celebration, is different now that your spouse
has died. The first time you experience those events
without your mate may be very difficult. I found that
often the anticipation of the upcoming event was more
ominous than the actual event.

Memories were just a glaring reminder of how empty
I felt. I walked out of church several times because a
song, message, or something else would trigger a painful
memory. On the date that would have been our twenty-
fifth wedding anniversary, I went to Leland, a special
haunt of ours, and reread love letters Rick had sent me
from Korea during our engagement. I sobbed and longed

for that time back again. But in doing that, I healed a little more.

About five or six months into grieving, a light came on while I was walking in my favorite woods. I was struck by the realization that no one else was going to take care of Susan; I needed to take care of myself. That realization helped immensely. Before that time, I had been in so much pain and had so little energy that I probably couldn't have taken control of my grief process. But the time had come.

I decided I needed to find other people who were in a similar profession who were also grieving. Maybe we could share our stories and experiences. So my search began—the search that eventually ended with coffee times with my coauthor, Bob, as well as other widows from the local chapter of Widowed Persons Services. Those conversations helped immensely. I found that others could relate to my experiences and feelings because they were also dealing with deep pain in losing a partner and were trying to cope as well. This realization helped me begin to break through my loneliness. I was on a search for Susan—a Susan without Rick. Who am I? Can my life, alone, go on and be good again? I began to believe it could.

I determined to do a number of things. In order to find myself, I needed to do all my favorite things again. I needed to visit my favorite vacation spots in Pentwater, Sanibel, and Mackinac Island. I needed to go to my favorite restaurants and see friends and family. And I needed to do it alone—without Rick. True, Rick and I had done these things together and had great times, but they were also a very real part of what I loved for myself. Doing these things was not always easy, but it helped me work through the pain, accept the fact that Rick was no longer with me, and figure out who I was as an individual in relation to these special places and people.

Grief and healing is difficult work, but I am so thankful I consciously made myself do it. At the time of the writing of this chapter, I was two and a half years beyond Rick's death, and I could truly say I had moved to the other side of grief. I was a whole person with warm and wonderful memories of over twenty-four years with someone I loved dearly—with whom I bore a daughter and with whom I shared life to the fullest. Now the pain is gone, but the memories live on. I had closed a volume of my life. After exploring the phase of widowhood and adjusting to being a single person, I am now remarried. I am happy and fulfilled, and I wish the same for you in whatever form that takes.

Bob's Story

Char died of ovarian cancer. The diagnosis was first made in the spring of 1990, just three days before Easter Sunday. She died three and a half years later following almost continuous chemotherapy, radiation, and five major surgeries. Her death was no surprise. We knew from the beginning that the survival rate for stage four ovarian cancer was less than 30 percent.

When Char died quietly that Sunday morning in October, I felt that an integral piece of me was ripped away. My first reaction was that I was seriously wounded—like a soldier in Vietnam. I was lying there wondering if I would emotionally bleed to death because this person whom I loved was ripped from me. How could I stop the bleeding? How could I heal the wound?

Over time I felt the loneliness; I felt the pain. But I wanted to get over it quickly. I hated grieving, but Char and I had been married for twenty-eight years. We had woven our lives together in an intricate and beautiful pattern. You just can't rip half of that tapestry away without it hurting the overall design.

I don't think it was a conscious decision on my part, but I suspect I adopted the same attitude toward the pain that I would have taken with respect to a broken leg: Give it time; it will heal. Like a wound, the body (and spirit) simply needs time. Grief will fix itself, just like a broken leg will finally heal.

I know now that this was not the best approach. A broken leg still needs the attention of a physician. The patient must engage in certain activities to aid the healing and must definitely avoid certain behaviors to insure that he doesn't cause more injury. But somehow, deep inside, I had confidence that the wound would heal. I didn't know when or how long it would take, but it would heal.

The second overwhelming reaction I had was the sense that my future (my life's plan) was also ripped from me. Char and I had dreamed and planned for a new life. We were nearing that point in our lives when the children would be leaving home. We could travel, pursue our ambitions to work overseas, and simply spend more time on our relationship. That was also ripped away. My future was gone. Hopes had died along with my wife.

I can see where I was functioning as a relatively typical male. My life was ordered. My work, spouse, family, and leisure were all in balance. Now one part was ripped away, seriously affecting the other components of my life. I thought all I needed was time to rebuild, to begin again. However, that was a daunting task. I wasn't always sure I was ready for it. Nearly eighteen months passed before I really took charge of my grieving process and began working toward full resolution.

How the Loss of a Spouse Is Expressed

Both men and women develop strong emotional ties with their spouse. True love does exist, and that love is experienced mutually between husband and wife. When a spouse dies, however, traditionally men and women express that grief differently.

Take emotions, for example. Men typically hide their emotions more than do women. They tend to internalize their feelings and, if they express them at all, do so in private. Women, on the other hand, tend to give more open expression to their feelings. Grief studies on gender differences among widowed persons indicate that about half of the men expressed their grief through crying whereas about three-fourths of the women did so.[1] The men who didn't cry admitted to getting choked up at times, suggesting that they were trying to squelch their emotions. Men often view control of their emotions as a strength or a virtue and are conditioned to think that tears are not very manly.

Expressing emotion, however, is an extremely healthy practice. Tears are a unique way of relieving tension. The old advice of "just have a good cry—you'll feel better" is, for the most part, true. Resisting the urge to cry or suppressing the emotions of grief can lead to the more serious psychological problem of clinical depression. After one year of being widowed, about half of both men and women report that they are not as down or depressed as they were previously.[2] Dealing with emotions as they occur is an effective way of dealing with grief.

A sense of guilt also usually accompanies the grief process. This feeling is often triggered by a variety of causes, including unfinished business with your spouse ("if only" theme), unresolved conflicts, or a sense that the surviving spouse didn't do enough ("I should have . . ."). Men differ from women, however, in that men either will not experience this feeling as intensely or the feeling won't last as long. Men typically are not as angry or hostile about their spouse's death, and they are less likely than women to think the death of their spouse was unfair. Men are conditioned to be practical and logical, and they are expected to move on quickly and not linger over their feelings. Men also seem to deal with their guilt more quickly. Women often experience an increase in their sense of guilt over time. By the end of the second month of grieving, most men say they have accepted the reality of their loss (an appropriate task of grieving), while most women are still acting as though their husband were still alive.

Grieving spouses can also express their grief through various rituals, ceremonies, and memorials. Men tend, however, to move through these activities quickly—attempting to get past them—while women view these events as significant milestones to be experienced more fully. Funerals, for example, are often events that a man wants to "get through." Following the funeral, they are unlikely to take the initiative to listen to a tape recording of the service. Women, on the other hand, tend to view the event more as a ceremony to which they might return with some regularity to think about and relive.

Both men and women have to face a number of firsts during the twelve months following their spouse's death. Men tend to attack these events as something to get through. Women will tend to focus on these events and ponder them even though they may be painful.

Some of the assignments suggested in this book may be especially difficult for a man. The assignments may not seem to have any practical or logical benefit, especially if (as a man) you just want to get on with it. We want to encourage you to take the time for these suggestions. Trust that symbolic memorials and other external demonstrations of your feelings are healthy ways to work through your grief and to reach a healthy resolution.

Susan's Story

Rick had been the one person with whom I shared my most intense emotional responses to life. We shared deeply about people, places, and events. I certainly talked with others about my feelings, but I was able to share my raw emotions with Rick without having to worry about reshaping or refining them to be socially acceptable. Now Rick was dead, and my primary emotional outlet was gone. I had no one to bounce things off. He and I had shared so many feelings and held so many views in common that I didn't know what I would do without him.

People who knew us viewed me as a strong and independent person, which is especially true in my professional life. But even I was surprised by how weak and ungrounded I felt when Rick died. Yet, except for a very few occasions, no one saw me cry. I was able to talk about how sad I felt, but I never got the impression that anyone really knew how desperate and awful I felt. Nor did they know how much energy it took for me to hold myself together. Yet almost every night for many months I would be home alone, sobbing, screaming, wailing. You name it—I allowed myself to express my feelings in their most raw form. I felt drained after that and would then journal, pray, or write Rick a letter. All of this helped reduce the emotional tension and agitation I felt.

Part of my hesitancy to display emotions is not only part of my genetics and environment, but it may also be a result of my profession. As a psychologist, others depend on me to model healthy ways to cope and adjust. Grieving was certainly appropriate, but I chose to express my grief in words, not in tears. Tears might make others too uncomfortable. That was fine with me, because I also didn't feel comfortable losing control of my emotions with most people. I did allow myself to express my feelings verbally and behaviorally—which is more important than where or with whom. Thinking back, it would have been nice to have had someone who could handle my weakness and vulnerability so I wouldn't have had to let go all by myself.

If you have someone with whom you can be completely open and vulnerable, consider yourself fortunate. Developing friendships with other widowed persons was a great help, and I will be forever grateful for the level of understanding I experienced with them. If you haven't tried to reach out to others who have recently lost a spouse, I certainly encourage you to begin doing that. Other widowed persons can be a valuable resource.

My daughter was the one person with whom I intentionally tried to express my feelings, even crying with her at times. I felt close to her and wanted to stay connected. She knew the pain we as a family had gone through, and she was also grieving and missing Rick. I wanted us to help each other grieve and to give each other permission to express that grief. However, as close as we felt to each other, no one can really know the essence of another person's relationship with someone else. They can't know exactly how the other person feels. Sarah and I both had our own grief to deal with, and as much as I wanted to help facilitate that for Sarah, I still don't know how successful I was. We can give our loved ones permission to grieve, but grief is still an individual journey for our children as well as for ourselves.

At the beginning I dealt with my grief by becoming very self-focused. I don't think I really saw anyone else's pain for a long time; mine was just too intense. I gave myself tasks that helped me grieve as well as provided me some physical release. I went on long walks in the woods or at the beach. I went to grief workshops, attended Widowed Person Services meetings, replayed tapes, looked at pictures, read letters, went skiing, biked, and hiked. All of the suggestions I have mentioned in this book, I did. And in time, combined with other grief work, I began to get through enough of the issues of loss that I started to feel better.

Widowed persons have many common feelings, largely because we all have had a significant personal relationship with someone who is no longer alive. The primary feeling with which I identify is losing a kindred spirit. But I also felt relief that the battle was over. I know that sounds like a strange combination—almost opposite ends of the spectrum. Nonetheless, grief doesn't have to make sense, nor do our feelings.

I am not aware of any feelings of guilt or remorse. Because of Rick's extended illness, we knew that he would eventually die. As a matter of fact, on three different occasions we really didn't think he would survive. But those experiences had a way of making us use every moment to its fullest. Rick and I did that in many ways. I had ample opportunity to express my love, ask for forgiveness, and insure that we did everything we wanted to do. Therefore, I have no "if only's" or "should have's" to deal with now. We lived our lives in the present, and I feel good about what we had and did. That may be true for you as well, especially if you knew your spouse was going to die and were able to talk about feelings, desires, and regrets. Once there is a resolution in a relationship, guilt doesn't have much chance of surviving.

By the time Rick died, I was no longer angry about his impending death except in one significant way. I was angry on behalf of my daughter. I was angry that she didn't have a dad anymore. I was angry that she didn't have a healthy dad for a good share of her life. I was angry that I no longer had Rick as a mutual parent who could enjoy our daughter with me. During his illness, I felt angry with the medical profession, with God, with Rick, and with others when I judged they weren't doing everything they could to help him on his journey. After he died, I realized that most of the anger was gone. If any anger or irritation lingered, it was directed mostly at those people who seemed to be ignorant or insensitive about how to help a grieving spouse. My tolerance level was quite low in dealing with people who had no way of knowing what being widowed was like. I have now come to realize that the missing ingredient is primarily education. Perhaps when we as widowed persons reach the other side of grief, we can participate in sharing our stories in order to help people better understand this journey through grief.

Bob's Story

I always thought I was a fairly open person emotionally. After all, as a pastor I have wept with those who weep and laughed with those who laugh. I am not afraid to shed a public tear on occasion, and I can also laugh boisterously.

As I review the initial weeks following Char's death, however, I recall clearly that I was acting as if I was the pastor helping someone else through a loss. I recall quite clearly several people commenting on how comforting I was to them at the funeral. Here I was, the surviving spouse, and I was comforting others in their grief! Only occasionally, when a very dear friend came by, would I begin to cry—but even then I was somewhat sharing in their tears.

For months after Char's funeral I would sit alone, as I had done for months before her death when she was hospitalized or asleep, listening to the Brooklyn Tabernacle Choir. Their version of "He's Been Faithful" and "Friend of a Wounded Heart" would trigger gushers of tears. I would cry, alone, for an hour at a time.

On other occasions, I would get angry. Some days I would be angry at God, other days at myself or at Char, but usually just plain angry at the whole rotten situation. I didn't ask for this, I didn't want it, and I wanted it to go away. Rarely would I tell anyone that. But I would go in my bedroom and throw pillows at the wall or take long walks (five miles or longer) just to release the anger.

I finally found release from the anger when I took charge of my grief. About eighteen months after Char died, I suddenly went into an intense period of grief again. Probably because I had taken such a passive attitude toward grief, many of the emotions had been stored deep inside. But I also finally realized that I had not died. My life was going to continue, and if there was to be any quality in my life, I had to do something about it. That's when I started doing a number of things: I realized I had put on weight because I had fallen into the trap of using food to make me feel better. I resolved to change my eating patterns, and over the next nine months I lost about fifteen pounds. I also started following many of the suggestions in this book, especially writing letters to Char and reading them to her at the cemetery. I retraced my steps to some of our favorite, sentimental places. I looked through pictures. But most of all I finished the remodeling of my kitchen. I had to move on. So I did all these things intentionally to say good-bye. I said good-bye a hundred times, but each time it got easier.

Now I know Char is gone. I loved her, but she is dead; I am not. I also love myself, and I will carry with me the wonderful memories of twenty-eight years of a happy marriage. The pain is finally gone. The memories are secure, and my life now goes on.

How the Loss of a Spouse Relates to Work or Career

Most men define themselves to some degree by their work or profession. When asked, "Who are you?" many men will answer with a reference to work. "I am a mailman," or "I am a teacher." For a man, career is one of the more powerful elements in defining himself.

For women, on the other hand, the definition of self comes from other sources. For many, the most powerful source is that of family or other significant relationships. With more women pursuing careers, this pattern may be changing. Yet for many women, their work is still often viewed as a supplement to that of their husband. Women may work, but men have careers. Just think, for example, who usually follows whom when a job transfer is made. Traditionally the wife will follow the husband. If the wife is to be transferred, she may be forced to switch jobs because the man's career has typically taken precedence.

When a partner's spouse dies, a man usually still has an established career as a point of reference and stability. "Well, at least I still have my job." A woman, however, often either has no lasting or defining career or may find that what she was doing will no longer be adequate to provide the financial resources necessary for her new life. This is exacerbated for a widow with children.

Both women and men may find work a distraction from the grieving process. Men especially are known to throw themselves into their work to avoid dealing with their loss. Women as well may use work to distract themselves from the pain and loneliness they are experiencing. You will need to find a balance here. Certainly, work can provide a needed respite from the pain of grieving. Work can help reduce physical and emotional tension and place you back into a more normal social setting. But you must be careful not to use work to avoid the tasks of grieving ahead of you.

Susan's Story

I think I exhibit more male characteristics with re-gard to career and work than the typical female. Per-haps twenty-five years ago that wasn't true. Then I viewed work as an adjunct, even unnecessary, compo-nent of my life. I had become a registered nurse and was teaching nursing. But when our daughter was born, I thought I would complete my master's degree largely as a stimulating outlet or diversion from parenting. I might return to work part time, I thought, after Sarah started going to school.

Then Rick was diagnosed with a brain tumor and was given five years to live. That changed things dramati-cally. I suddenly realized I was the one who would have to provide the financial support. I went through a process similar to women who were widowed and didn't have a career, suddenly facing the brute fact that fi-nancial stability rests on their shoulders. My advantage was that I had a warning; I could prepare.

So I did go back to school—not as a diversion or an outlet but for financial survival. I not only completed a master's degree but also a doctorate in psychology. When Rick died, I had already been employed as a full-time clinical psychologist for six years. I had always loved my work and found the profession not only in-triguing but an excellent diversion to my personal life. I had developed the capacity to compartmentalize my life so I could leave my home life behind when I went into the office. I would go into my work mode (and still do, by the way) in which I totally engrossed myself in work issues, leaving personal and family issues behind.

When Rick died and Sarah was away at college, I was tempted to avoid the pain by simply staying in this other world of work. After all, my personal life was now empty, lonely, and totally unpleasant. But I knew better. I knew and had told many clients that immersing yourself in work doesn't heal the hurt or resolve the loss. It only postpones the inevitable. So I forced myself to go home at night, refusing to extend my work schedule to fill the loneliness and the massive hole left by Rick's death. I made the conscious decision not to distract or bury myself in my work.

Weekends were extremely difficult times. At first I kept busy with family and friends who surrounded me, often letting them take charge of my life and schedule on the weekends. But then I realized that some of those activities felt more uncomfortable than simply staying at home. Staying at home seemed easier than going out and having to deal with others while I was still in pain. So I spent time at home by myself, and eventually I realized I could use these weekends to work through my grief. So on Saturdays and Sundays I pored over slide trays and picture albums. I began to do more of the activities I mentioned earlier. And eventually I came to recognize more clearly the positive effects of balancing work and personal time in moving through my grief.

Bob's Story

I think I am a hard worker. While Char was healthy, I managed to work hard both as a pastor and later as a teacher. Along with my career, I finished three graduate degrees concurrently with my work. Char finished her master's degree, and we raised three active children.

When Char's health was failing and we needed time to see doctors or travel to other cities for treatment, or

when she needed to undergo surgery with long recu-
peration periods, I still managed somehow to keep on
teaching. I owe a lot to my seminary for their flexibil-
ity in scheduling.

As I look back, I can see how I was using my teaching as one way of maintaining a semblance of structure
and order in my life. But as Char weakened and I pulled
back from my work emotionally and mentally, I knew
that after she died I would have to make up for it. I owed
it to the seminary. They were being lenient with me,
so I had to pay them back. Soon after Char died, I began
pouring myself into my work. I needed to fill my hours,
and work served as a good diversion since I could stay
at the office rather than facing an empty house. Week-
days were okay because I had something to do, but
weekends were murder. I was alone and especially aware
that my kindred spirit was no longer with me.

I also kept busy in other ways. We had purchased
our old home in 1980, ten years before Char's diagnosis. I'm fairly handy around the house, and during those
ten years I had refurbished, repainted, remodeled, and
redone nearly everything in that house. In late August
1993, when Char was finally confined to a hospital bed
in our home and unable to move around because of her
extremely weakened condition, I started remodeling
the upstairs bathroom. I stripped it down to the studs,
put in a new tub/shower, and redecorated. I did it for
Char. She had always wanted it done, and I wanted
the project finished before she died. I finished the job,
but Char never saw it. She was too weak even to be
carried upstairs. I took pictures; that was the best I
could do.

About three months after Char's death, I started remodeling the kitchen—a major project. Again, I ripped
the entire kitchen and eating room apart. I knocked out

a closet, redefined space, installed a new bay window, and totally modernized the kitchen. All of the time, I was conscious that I was fulfilling another dream Char and I had together. I justified the project on the basis that it would be good for resale. But I really knew I was doing it for her. Sometimes I would imagine what she would say when she saw it, only to remember that she would never see it.

Ending the kitchen project triggered for me the beginning of a real healing. I had successfully delayed my grieving, but now I couldn't avoid her absence any longer. I had to face my fears, my emotions, and my emptiness. I was tired of living for the past; now I had to move on. Perhaps some of us men feel we have to pay our dues before moving on. I had paid mine. The project was done. Now I could work on myself.

How Others React to the Loss

One of the most difficult aspects of grieving is shifting one's perspective concerning previous social relationships. Friendships change—that is a simple fact. A person who has been married and had a number of married friends now has to learn to relate to them as a single person. Initially good friends come to the rescue, but remember, they are grieving too. When they see you, they often still see your spouse as well. They want to help. What shape this help takes, however, is often conditioned by gender.

Many people see women as needing relief from their daily tasks in order to attend to their feelings. Friends believe widows need emotional support because they have been abandoned. They also need someone to do some of the more typical male tasks such as help with finances, cars, or lawn care. Friends, parents, and/or children will tend to assume certain roles they thought your husband performed—especially the roles associated with protection and security.

Men, on the other hand, are often treated as if they have few emotional needs. Friends and helpers often focus more on the man's physical needs. They are concerned about how he will provide for his meals, do his laundry, and (especially if there are children at home) perform all the other domestic tasks normally done by his wife.

This makes grieving especially difficult for men. Because men tend to avoid expressing their emotions openly, they need encouragement to do so. Now we see that friends also tend to avoid reference to the emotional side. Some studies indicate that two months after a spouse's death, less than one-third of the men had talked directly to someone else about their wife's death. This is compared to over one-half of the women.[3] Since men are so unlikely to communicate their feelings, finding a support system is important. If you are a widower, we encourage you to overcome what may be a natural tendency to isolate yourself. Seek out a close friend or join a support group where you can safely give expression to your feelings. The good news is that by the end of the first year of grieving, almost three-fourths of the men and over 90 percent of the women had asked for help in some form.[4] The bottom line is to take the initiative. Ask for help. In most cases, your friends may not know what kind of help you really need. Talk with them about the kind of support and help that would be the best for you.

Susan's Story

When Rick was ill and dying in the late summer and fall of 1994, our family and friends were available whenever I needed them. That felt so supportive. When he died, they were also there. They were grieving too, but even in their grief they conveyed the message that they cared about Sarah and me.

Reality began to hit for me, however, after the burial. We came back from the cemetery to my house for lunch. As family and friends began to leave, I had an urge to stop them. I didn't want them to go. I would be left to sit with my grief alone. The pain had been muted before, thanks to their presence, but now the house was empty. Soon Sarah and her boyfriend would also leave, and I would be left alone with my raw pain.

I began to experience that family and friends can provide support to some degree, but fundamentally this was my journey. I couldn't put it in words then, but as I look back I now realize that was the first clue. Over the course of grieving, I felt friends soothe me for the short time I was with them, but most of the time I was alone. Friends were there only for a fleeting sliver of time. For the rest of the time, I had to deal with me.

My parents have always been a close and important part of my life. Much earlier we had changed from a parent-child to a healthy adult-adult relationship. I liked that. When Rick died, we needed to revisit the dynamics of our relationship. They obviously cared so much about me that they wanted to fill the ugly hole left by Rick's death. They had loved Rick too and were also grieving. The temptation was to allow them to fill the gap—to take up some of the space left by Rick's death. They were willing to spend time with me on those lonely weekends. At first that looked attractive—a good distraction and time filler. But somehow in my grief I sensed that it wouldn't be healthy in the long run for either of us, so I started to set some boundaries for myself about how much contact I would have with them. I think that was difficult for all of us, and perhaps even puzzling and hurtful at first for them, but I couldn't allow my time to be filled with all those activities because I would be avoiding the pain of grief I so desperately had to face. In retrospect, I think that was a wise decision. My relation-ship with my parents has returned to a comfortable adult-adult relationship. I don't depend on them, but I do enjoy their company. You may also be dealing with a family who wants to try to make things better for you. I hope you can make wise choices in setting boundaries so you will not be diverted from your primary goal of getting to the other side of grief.

I also hadn't thought much about how friendships might change after Rick died. I think I assumed they would just continue. But without Rick, I quickly felt different when friends asked me over for dinner. The empty chair was screaming out Rick's absence. Some-thing's different—someone's missing! Facing the real-ity that I was no longer a couple was very difficult. Over time, being with old friends became easier, but after the busyness of the holidays was past, I noticed that peo-ple were calling less frequently. I wasn't sure why.

I went to my first Widowed Persons Services meet-ing three months after Rick died. They were discussing the topic "Changing Friendships." Someone made the comment that after the first year of widowhood, many old friendships simply won't be there anymore. I re-member thinking how that surely wouldn't be true for me and my friends. I felt anxious about relationships changing; they were all I had. However, over the course of the years since Rick died, the contours of many of my friendships have changed. They have not neces-sarily ended, but they look and function somewhat dif-ferently. At times the adjustment was hurtful. Some-times I even began to think that some of my friends had been more interested in Rick than in me. However, I also learned the value of developing new friendships, especially with other unmarried people and those going through similar experiences. Although I have valued friends who have been divorced, I still wanted to spend time with people who were widowed—people who typically missed their spouses and their relationship with them rather than feeling some relief or happiness that a marriage was over. Now I have come to the point, however, that it really doesn't matter any longer if my friends are married, divorced, or widowed simply because I am able to see myself as a complete person who was fortunate to have had a good marriage for twenty-four years and is now beginning another volume.

Bob's Story

I don't think I really let very many people get close to me emotionally for the first year after Char's death. My children and I would have some talks, but they were usually brief and guarded. They had their own pain; how could I burden them with mine? Other friends cared about me very much, but they were simply not around when I really felt like talking. My extended family and my friends probably would have been willing to help, but I kept my grief inside until late at night. You don't bother friends late at night. Occasionally I would talk to a friend or two about my situation, but for the most part, I handled it alone.

One of the reasons I protected myself, I believe, was that all my other friends were grieving too. I think they found it hard to accept me or see me as a person in my own right. Especially during the first year after Char died, they saw me as "alone" or "a widower" or "hurting." I don't think they could just see me as "Bob" without the shadow of Char by my side.

Only when I began to meet new friends who were not part of my prior history did I start to feel valued for myself. Ironically, I was much better able to talk about my grief with them because they could focus on my grief without having it confused with their own. If I had to do it again, I would have reached out sooner. I might have gone to a support group; I might have tried to find other grieving persons who had not known Char so their grief would not complicate the matter.

When the numbers change (from two to one), friendships change. They just do. They can be redefined or reaffirmed, but they change. Real friends recognize that. Some friends may remain close to you even in your singleness, but remember that we go through a number of phases in our lives, and some friends are there only during one of those periods. There are many potential new friends out there whom you can meet.

Views on Sex and Remarriage

Society holds many distorted views on sex and remarriage for widows and widowers. Many people find it very hard to disassociate themselves from their deceased spouse because marriage was such a defining power in their life.

Widows, more than widowers, tend to feel a strong sense of loyalty to their deceased spouses and are very concerned about how their behavior might look to others. Because women tend to define themselves by personal or social relationships, they may find it harder to disassociate themselves from their deceased husband.

Men, on the other hand, tend to move on more quickly into a sexual or marriage relationship. Men want to rebuild their life's structure. They tend to want to return to their previously balanced life by reestablishing an orderly home, decreasing their loneliness, and satisfying their sexual desires. These desires push them toward social recovery more quickly than women, although they tend to be slower with their emotional recovery.

Achieving social recovery does not necessarily mean remarriage. We will deal with the issue of remarriage more extensively in chapter 9. Understand, however, that remarriage is only one way of reestablishing a stable life pattern. The differences between men and women are quite sharp on this issue of remarriage. About 65 percent of men compared with 45 percent of women said early in their bereavement that they would miss a sexual relationship. By the end of the first year of grief, about half of the men were either remarried or in a serious relationship. Only 18 percent of the widows were in any type of committed relationship.[5] Of course, this statistic is also influenced by the fact that there are far fewer men available than women. Some studies indicate that women may have a greater level of fear or anxiety about establishing a new relationship than do men.[6] Coming to the point of accepting yourself as a sexual being is also an important aspect of the grieving process.

Susan's Story

I never planned to get married again. I doubt that anyone who is recently widowed does. I remember especially clearly a sunny afternoon in the summer prior to Rick's death. We were sitting on our porch overlooking the lake, and Rick obviously had an agenda. He surprised me by his persistence in talking about what my life would be like when he was dead. I didn't want to think about life without him, and as he was talking I clung to him, begging him not to talk about his not being around anymore. He became irritated, sternly saying that he needed to say some things to me regardless of how much I didn't want to hear them. He continued on in spite of my protests. He said he loved being married to me, and he thought I made a great marriage partner. As a result, he thought I belonged in a relationship again, and that he didn't want to think of me without having a soul mate. He spoke of how he was pained that he couldn't remain with me and be that partner, but he wanted me to promise that I would remarry.

I can clearly recall my repulsion at his words and telling him that I would never remarry, but he persisted by saying that remarrying would honor him because people who are happy in a marriage do remarry if the opportunity presents itself. He didn't give up until I promised him that if the right person came along, I would remember his wishes and remarry. At the time (and for a long time later) I still believed I would not have to keep that promise because no one could possibly come into my life that I would want to marry—much less someone who might want to marry me. Not that I thought I was unlovable, but I knew I had an unusually special man in Rick, and I didn't believe I would ever find another special person. A close friend of mine reinforced that notion when I expressed sadness that I would never have another partner. This friend agreed with me that it was highly unlikely I would remarry because my standards were too high. I just never could see myself with anyone else. I admit that I hated parts of being alone—not having a kindred spirit, going to bed by myself, and at times feeling sexually frustrated. But I tried to sublimate those desires into other areas of my life.

About six months after Rick died, I decided to attempt to develop new friendships (both male and female) to help fill some of the empty space in my life. In the process of doing that, I was able to better see myself as a single adult. But before I ever reached a point where I wanted to date, I met Bob. He and I began to develop a friendship based on helping each other through our grief processes. That friendship grew, and after the first anniversary of Rick's death, we began dating. We then began to work on blending our families, which is an art form in itself—something akin to playing chess. How much simpler our first marriages were without complicated roles and relationships to deal with. Our family and friends are adjusting at their own paces. We feel blessed and joyful about beginning a new volume in our lives. We were married in August 1997. Life does move on after the hurt and pain of grief. Good can come from bad. There is a new morning after mourning.

Bob's Story

Char and I talked a lot about her death and about what my life might be like after she died. She was very open about her desires. She could usually accept the reality of her impending death because spiritually she was right with God. Her faith was strong, and she was getting very tired of the pain and weakness that had invaded her body. For the last two months she asked me to pray that she would die soon.

Char deeply regretted that she would not be around for her children's weddings and the birth of her grandchildren. Since her death, all three children have married, and the first grandchild was born—Hannah Charlene.

Char insisted that I should remarry. She only had two requests: that I wait at least one year and that I not marry a certain divorcée whom Char thought had eyes for me. But she gave me permission to move on, though at the time I thought the idea to be totally adulterous. I resisted her urging several times, but she insisted so often that finally I simply thanked her for the permission but reaffirmed that the issue of remarriage was a long way down the road.

During the early winter months following Char's death, I had to make a decision about a headstone for her grave. My parents had purchased a joint headstone and placed it on my father's grave even though my mother did not die for another ten years. I went to the monument company to investigate options. "Yes," they said, "we can certainly design a double marker with your name on it as well as hers." "Yes," they said, "we can put an eagle on it with Char's favorite verse." No one bothered to ask me if I really wanted a double marker. No one talked about the pros and cons of such a choice. So I ordered a double marker—my name to appear on the left side without the date of death inscribed; Char's name would be on the right side.

When I made my early visits to the cemetery, I took some comfort in that joint headstone. But by mid summer (six months after her death), I had a growing discomfort seeing my name etched in that stone. This was her grave, not mine. Certainly, I fully intended at that time to be interred beside her when I died, but I became increasingly aware that I had not died. This was not my grave plot—at least not yet. I had too much living to do. I wanted the headstone to memorialize Char, but now it began to represent more than I had intended. The headstone seemed to say that I was to continue some form of relationship with my deceased wife. But as the grave site lost a sense of her presence (as the grief process progresses, the survivor often detaches emotionally from the physical grave site), I began to realize I had made a mistake in ordering a double headstone. This was the beginning of my awakening. The decision to replace the joint headstone with a single one was extremely difficult. I had to be clear to myself that I was not rejecting my past memories of my deceased wife, but I also had to be clear that my identity was not found engraved on a stone in a cemetery. I have a new life. I am moving on.

When I die, I may well be buried by Char, but I may not be. What I do know is that a joint headstone suggests that I can somehow continue to have a relationship with someone who has died, but that is impossible. So the stone was changed—not because I am rejecting anything of the past, but because the headstone does not represent my future. "Until death do us part" is what the wedding vows were. Death has parted us. A headstone should not keep us together. I am free to move on, free to live and love again.

Another part of the awakening that I went through eighteen months after Char died was connected with a reawakening of my sexual side. I began to realize that the intimacy I once had within marriage was something I would yearn to have again if the circumstances were right. I couldn't imagine spending the rest of my life alone for a number of reasons, including giving expression to my sexuality.

Yet I had no desire to date—that sounded adolescent. I wanted friends first. Later, perhaps, I would consider remarriage. In a conversation with my brother, I spelled out my conditions for a possible mate. They were very high expectations—so high he thought them to be nearly impossible. But that was all right with me. I had a good marriage once, and if I were to marry again, I would want nothing less.

Susan and I met in the spring of 1995. We became friends; neither of us had romantic intentions or ambitions. Rick had died only six months earlier. I was still going through my awakening. But we became kindred spirits. We started talking about writing this book, and then we began working on the manuscript. It wasn't until November of 1995 that we started dating. Even then we were both cautious. Each respected the other's need to totally resolve any grief issues before moving on. As friends we have helped each other immensely. We will be friends forever, even within our marriage.

Be Your Own Person

We hope you can find yourself somewhere in these stories. We are not typical—no one is. That is our point. You
are who you are, whether you are a man or a woman. Certainly, gender plays a very important part in shaping your
perception of yourself. Many studies point out that men
and women are not only physically but psychologically different. As apparent as their physical differences may be, so
also men and women possess different emotional and psychological features.

However, all male or female characteristics are general-
ities. We are each unique human beings, and some men
and women possess the qualities often assigned to the opposite gender. Characteristics defined as feminine or mas-
culine do not belong exclusively to one or the other gender; they belong to all of us. We firmly believe that especially
in the grieving process, both men and women can benefit
greatly by embracing the characteristics of the opposite
gender in addition to those of their own.

7

How Can You Be a Grieving Parent?

Dealing with Children on the Journey

If you have children at home after your spouse died, you face an especially difficult situation. You face the double task of dealing with your own grief and helping your children deal with their grief. How can you find a balance between these two extremely important but emotionally draining tasks? What are some things you can do to help you on this journey? Are there obstacles you need to avoid?

The Psychologist Says

When we truly care for ourselves, it becomes possible to care far more profoundly about other people. The more alert and sensitive we are to our

143

own needs, the more loving and generous we can be toward others.

Eda LeShan

Dealing with a Child's Grief

Children need to grieve, but you should be aware that they do not express their grief in the same way as adults. As a surviving parent, you are a role model for your children. They will watch closely how you express your emotions, deal with anger, manage daily tasks, and deal with issues of faith. With respect to emotions, for example, if you let your children see your sadness, you show them it is okay to display painful emotions. Your children may tend to imitate your style of grieving, and it is important to help them express their feelings rather than internalize them.

Be careful, however, to maintain a balance. If your children suspect you are so grief stricken that you are not able to handle any more, they may not want to burden you with their own grief. Children are usually aware that you are the only parent left, and they don't want you to become so overburdened that you can't function. However, they will naturally make more demands on your time because their other parent has died. You will have to find time away from your children to deal with your own grief so you can also properly manage your expression of grief in front of your children.

A child's grief is often complicated by unspoken fears. Your children may feel guilty about their parent's death. They may have some mistaken notion of magic or wish fulfillment, thinking that their angry thought or wish actually caused the death of their parent. They may also have some regret for the way they treated their deceased parent. Children may even believe their parent's death was a result of or punishment for their misbehavior. Children need help in understanding that they had no part in their parent's death. Give them a clear explanation that the death occurred because of an illness or accident. Help them understand the reality that these things happen in this world. You also may want to share with them that all of us will die sometime; we just don't know when or how it will happen.

Honesty in explaining a parent's death is essential. Don't try to shelter your children from the reality of death. Telling children something that is inaccurate or so general that it is misleading will not help and could cause your children to lose trust in you. Avoid using terminology that refers to the deceased parent as "gone," "asleep," "lost," or "passed away." Euphemisms are confusing. Tell your children that their parent died and is no longer with you. The amount and detail you share needs to be appropriate to your children's ages and their questions, but whatever you say, make certain it is true.

As a Christian, you may wish to reassure your children that they may see each other in heaven someday. But even in describing heaven, be on guard to represent the Bible accurately. We know a lot about heaven, but none of us knows exactly what it will be like. The Bible is especially unclear about the nature of family relationships. Keep the ultimate focus on the fact that heaven is a place of perfection, and we know that those who are in heaven with God experience greater happiness and pleasure than we will ever have on earth.

HELPFUL SUGGESTIONS

1. Spend some time one-on-one with each of your children expressing your sadness that your spouse and your child's parent died.

> Allow the child to see some appropriate emotional expressions of grief from you.
> 2. Allow your children to ask questions about their parent's death. Reassure them of their noninvolvement in this event—death happens, and no one causes it.

Dealing with the Issue of Emotional Security

Parents provide their children with emotional security. When one of the parents dies, the children's needs for safety and security are intensified. Your children need to know that you are there for them, that you will listen and accept whatever they need to say, and that their lives will still be stable and secure. One essential element of providing this security is a continuous expression of your love for your children. Give your children frequent hugs.

Try to maintain as much of the normal routine as possible. Be especially careful that your children are not tempted to assume roles and responsibilities previously performed by your spouse. Some children feel the need to do this; other surviving parents sometimes expect this to happen. But the last thing children need is to feel burdened with the responsibilities of the parent who died. Too often children are told that now they will need to be the "little man" or "little woman" of the household. This is extremely damaging and inappropriate. Yet if you feel too overwhelmed to find time for your children, they may be tempted to be "mommy" or "daddy" just to get your attention or to help you so you may be able to find more time for them. If you sense this happening, ask for help from family or friends until you can decide how to manage or rearrange the load on an ongoing basis. Most of us typically don't have the extra time to take on more duties when our spouse dies. Reprioritizing some of your tasks and responsibilities will probably be necessary.

You can also provide security by maintaining your contacts with family and friends. Your children are accustomed to seeing and having a certain group of family and friends interact with them. If your children see that these people are also grieving, it will reassure them that what they are experiencing is normal. This may also remind your children that they still have a foundation of support from people who care about them.

Children often see parents as immortal and infallible. It is very frightening for children to learn that their parents are human and die. Your children counted on their deceased parent to be there, and they feel the loss or sense of abandonment just as much as you do. Eventually your children will learn that change is really the only constant in life, but that awareness comes with age and maturity. Before then, your children need the security that you (and extended family and friends) must now continue to provide without the assistance of their other parent. With that reassurance, hopefully you can all develop a positive perspective as you get to the other side of grief.

Frequently reinforce the fact that your children's deceased parent loved them, and remind your children of the pride and joy their parent found in them and that they can have from their memories of that relationship. Help them form and articulate their memories, and assist them in choosing pictures or other keepsakes that will be concrete symbols of that relationship.

> ### Helpful Suggestions
> 1. Take time each day to express love and caring for your children through hugging and telling them of your love.
> 2. Plan a time every week or two during which you do something fun alone with each of your children for a few hours.
> 3. Help your children develop a memory book or box of keepsakes that are reminders of their deceased parent. Encourage them to write or draw about their memories.

Dealing with Grief at Different Ages

Each child is an individual, so they need to be dealt with as unique beings. However, children in certain age groups may have similar responses to death and grief because of their cognitive and psychological development. Keep the children's ages and capacities in mind when answering their questions.

Prior to the age of three, you may find it hard to explain death to your child because of his or her limited verbal and thinking skills. A six-month-old has *label object constancy*, meaning the baby is able to keep an object in mind when out of sight. By the age of two years, a child has some concept of death through their experiences with animals. Children at this age see death as meaning that the object doesn't move. They have little understanding or appreciation for the permanency of death. Because they cannot verbalize their thoughts and feelings, very young children will probably be clingy. Their anxiety and insecurity may even precipitate some developmental regression for a brief period of time.

A preschooler between the ages of three and five still cannot grasp the finality or inevitability of death. They tend to believe death is temporary and reversible—the person who died is simply living under different circumstances. This age group is concrete, literal, direct, and curious. They believe the world revolves around them. A typical question from a three- to five-year-old might be, "How can he breathe?" or, "When is she going to be alive again?" At this age, children tend to have short attention spans, so responses to their questions should be brief, concrete, and repetitive.

Six- and seven-year-olds are beginning to understand that the death of their parent is irreversible, but they cannot yet conceptualize their own death. They may see death as a person who takes other people away if they don't run fast enough to escape. Children of this age may have difficulty expressing themselves verbally about death, so it may help to have them draw pictures and then ask them to describe what's happening. Sometimes when these children ask questions, you may not understand what they are really asking. Try to clarify their questions by first asking what they think. Their questions still tend to be quite literal, and also graphic. For example, they may ask if worms will get to the person in the grave. Watch for an emerging sense of guilt in children from one to seven years old. They also have a tendency to feel insecure, assuming that if their parent died, they might die too—as if death were contagious like a cold.

By the time children reach ages seven to nine they begin to recognize that death is inevitable and suspect it may also happen to them. This age group usually deals with death better than any other age group, probably because they tend to readily accept most things. They have an active fantasy life and wonder about the dead body and what happens to it. Drawing pictures may serve as a healthy outlet for expressing their feelings.

Children between the ages of ten and twelve will probably recognize that death will certainly occur to them as well, but not until they are very old. As a result, they usually don't worry about it. Note that they also may think death happens as a punishment for those who have done bad things and may be questioning their parent's death from that perspective. Because they are beginning to develop the capacity to reason, children of this age are also more open to and concerned about the spiritual dimensions of death. They are also beginning to think abstractly and may want to know more about the meaning of funerals.

If you are reading this prior to your spouse's funeral, think about how you might involve your children in the visitation and the funeral. Protecting your children by isolating them from these activities is not psychologically healthy. Children internalize what they are capable of understanding and will ask questions if they want more input. Certainly younger children should not be expected to participate in the total visitation, but you may want to consider having them there for a short time, especially if they can be with family or close friends.

Youth between thirteen and eighteen years of age will usually have the most difficult time with death and grieving. Their lives are already in a period of extreme change, and teenagers typically are confused about their emotions and are embarrassed to ask questions. They tend to avoid talking about feelings with anyone and often turn to their peer group for support rather than a parent. But most of their peers are incapable of being supportive because of their own tendency to be self-focused. Emotional reactions are at an all-time high for teenagers, and their grief reactions tend to be more intense than those of adults. Most adolescents do not allow themselves to go through the grief process at the time of their parent's death. Grieving gets delayed and complicated because of the multiple pressures of adolescence—the need to conform to their peer group, the need to be cool, or any number of other developmental tasks. On top of this, because your teenager is an emerging adult, you may be more tempted to expect your teenager to take over some of the roles and responsibilities of your deceased spouse. Be very careful to avoid this.

Adolescents are prone to periods of depression. Watch for changes in behavior, especially continual withdrawal and isolation, discontinuing normal activities such as sports, avoiding friends, or a disinterest or drop in academic performance. Adolescents already have a higher rate of suicide than the general population, and a major loss could trigger a suicidal tendency in some teens. Try to talk with your teenagers about their feelings and reasons for hope as life continues. If you believe your teen is depressed, counseling is the appropriate course to take.

Beyond the age of eighteen, your adolescents have actually become young adults. They typically have more diversion in their lives, but this doesn't mean they are not grieving. If this young adult is in college, some of the pressure to conform still exists. Even though persons in this age group are developing more maturity, college life can be distracting and demanding, overshadowing doing grief work.

As the years go by, your adult children may long to have their deceased parent with them at college graduation, when they land their first real job, get married,

or have their own children. At each significant mile-
stone, the loss of their parent will need to be revisited.

HELPFUL SUGGESTIONS

1. Make certain you, as the surviving parent,
   understand where each of your children is
   in their age-appropriate development before talking with them about the death and
   answering questions.
2. Help your children understand the deceased parent's death from their own age
   perspective through various explanations
   and books.[1]
3. Recognize that as your children age, they
   will probably need to discuss the death again
   from a different or more sophisticated, abstract perspective. Allow time around each
   birthday to reevaluate where your child is
   in understanding the death and what may
   be necessary to revisit in more depth.

Questions Your Child Might Ask

Being prepared is always the best option. Regardless
of what age your children may be, you can anticipate
the kind of questions they might ask as they work
through grief with you. Here are some sample questions
that children might ask. Think about how you would
answer them if your child were asking you.

What is *dead*, or what does *dead* mean?
What made him or her die?
Where is he or she now?

Can he or she see me?
How long will my mom or dad be dead?
Can it happen to you or me?
How will I manage without my mom or dad?
Who will take care of me?

Prepare yourself in advance for these questions, and re-member to answer them honestly, directly, and specif-ically. Older children may wonder about the spiritual dimension and role of God in causing or preventing the death if religious beliefs have been taught previously.

After the death of your spouse and your children's parent, you will need to do a lot of work both for your-self and with your children. Your family will undergo a metamorphosis; you will need to form a new, functional family with you as the surviving parent at the helm. This will be a major adjustment for both you and your children. As a single parent you will need to be wise in deciding how you are going to manage your former part-ner's role in addition to your own. This doesn't mean you do it all—that would probably be impossible and certainly not the healthiest choice. Your spouse may have had skills and interests you don't have. Your hus-band may have enjoyed playing ball in the yard with your children, or your wife may have been teaching your daughter how to sew. You may not naturally choose these activities for yourself. You will need to discuss with your children how to handle the hole that is now left because a parent died. If your children still want to pursue a certain activity, you may find a friend or rela-tive who could help.

Remember that two parents can naturally cover twice the territory in transporting, assisting, and sup-porting children. You are now parenting alone, and you need to be realistic. You need to downsize in the areas you and your children think are less important. Choose one activity that each child values highly, and limit yourselves to that one. Let the rest go. You will quickly learn that we often try to cram far too many things into our lives, thinking somehow that more is better. We often find out too late that *more* tends to crowd out the important things. Having time with your children regardless of the activity is far better than running from one thing to another. Now is the time to simplify—both for your sake as well as that of your children.

Helpful Suggestions

1. Prior to explaining your partner's death to your children, it will be necessary to clearly understand your own thoughts and beliefs about death. Use this time as a reaffirmation and grounding for yourself.
2. Identify your priorities in parenting your children and what involvements you want to continue for them based on the realities of being a single parent.
3. Evaluate from a time perspective what you did directly for your children and what your partner contributed. List each task and the time involved. Consider now what is realistic for you to handle, what can be reassigned to someone else, and what may need to be discontinued (at least for the time being). This is where friends and family may be invaluable in helping with transportation, practicing, etc. Then sit down with your children and decide together what is important and realistic to continue and which activities need to be eliminated.

The Pastor Says

Unless you change and become like little children, you will never enter the kingdom of heaven.

Matthew 18:3

Let the little children come to me, and do not hinder them, for the kingdom of heaven belongs to such as these.

Matthew 19:14

Separating Fact from Fiction

Now I lay me down to sleep,
I pray the Lord my soul to keep.
If I should die before I wake,
I pray the Lord my soul to take.

You may have prayed that prayer as a child. Perhaps you also taught the prayer to your own children. But have you ever really thought about what you are asking your child to say in that prayer? Certainly, many of us have used a little prayer like this to give our children some assurance that even as they sleep God is watching over them. Smaller children often go through a stage in which they fear the dark, think that ghosts are in the closet, or believe a monster is under their bed. So we teach them the prayer. The question is, does it really allay their fears or does it get them thinking about death just before they go to bed? We must be careful, therefore, to avoid making too close of a connection between sleep and death.

Children's attitudes toward dying and death are easily influenced by their parents. How you manage your

grief will greatly influence how your children will manage theirs. But it is also important to separate fact from
fiction.

Fact: God doesn't want people to die any more than
we do. Death was not part of God's original design for
this world, and death will also not be part of the new
heaven and new earth he will create when Christ returns. Death is part of the curse of sin, and it represents
evil. While God indeed rescues us from death, we must
be careful to communicate clearly to our children that
death itself is not what God intended, for God is good.

Perhaps you can use an analogy to help smaller children understand this. If you are building a sand castle
by the shoreline, you try to make the nicest castle you
can. Just when you finish, a huge wave comes and breaks
down part of the castle. The wave was not something
you intended to happen, but you start again. You begin
to rebuild—perhaps this time with an even better plan
than before. In some ways death is like the wave that
unexpectedly rushes over us. Death wasn't what God
originally meant to have happen, but it did. He allows
that to happen, but he can still rebuild, and often he
can rebuild in ways far better than we could imagine.

Fact: Death is real; it happens to every living thing.
We live in a culture that so worships life that we have
almost denied the natural cycle of life and death. While
death wasn't first intended, death still is part of living.
Flowers grow in the spring; they die in the fall. Turtles
live just so long in their terrarium, and they die. Pets
live; pets die. Children know that. They only need help
in facing this reality directly.

One of the best ways to help children face the reality of death is to talk to them directly about it. Use the
word *death* rather than some euphemism like *gone away*
or *isn't here any longer.* Children need to understand

that the death of their parent is not the same as when visitors leave to go home. Their parent is not coming back for another visit sometime. You may think that is cruel, but actually such straight talk is the most helpful. The Bible doesn't downplay the reality of death; neither should we.

Fact: Death isn't just the end of one thing, it is the beginning of something else. In some ways children can believe in life-after-death much more easily than adults. They still have the capacity to look beyond the physical world because their imaginations still allow them to go places adults fear to go. Heaven is a real place, but we adults must admit that we really don't know very much about it. Our minds are also filled with speculations: How old will we be in heaven? If I die at the age of six, will I be that age for all eternity? Will I recognize my parents? Will husbands and wives still have an intimate relationship different from other relationships? We don't know. The Bible doesn't give us specific answers to those questions.

Children also have specific questions: Will my deceased mom or dad know if I do well on my Little League team? Will he or she know if I do something wrong? Can my mom or dad see me? Can he or she hear me? These types of questions are difficult to answer, but it is good to help children understand the truth of their deceased parent's relationship with them. If it was true, let them know that their parent loved them deeply, cared for them very much, and will still love them very much in heaven. But you need to be realistic as well and avoid using a deceased parent as some sort of threat and/or reward for your children's present behavior.

The parent's death is the time for a new beginning, not just for the deceased in some spiritual sense of the word, but also for the survivors. Your children must be helped to accept the fact that the deceased parent will not be here for them. Pride in their accomplishments and celebrations of special events like graduations or proms must come from the living. Children must learn, even as you must learn, that they have a different life to live now. This new reality isn't something they wanted, but they need to begin to rebuild their own lives just as they would rebuild the sand castle that was wiped out by a wave.

Childlike Faith

How, then, can you best deal with the spiritual nature of your children's journey back to wholeness and health following the death of a parent? In his ministry, Jesus adopted a unique attitude to children—especially unique for the culture in which he was living. He not only accepted children into his ministry, but he used them as an example of true faith. He multiplied a small boy's bread and fish to feed a hungry crowd (John 6:1–15). Even near the end of his life, he chided his disciples for trying to chase the children away. "Let the little children come to me, and do not hinder them," he said, "for the kingdom of God belongs to such as these" (Mark 10:14). And earlier in his ministry Jesus said that unless we have faith like that of a child, we will not enter the kingdom of heaven (Matt. 18:3). Let's look briefly at both of these issues.

First, Jesus accepted at face value the faith and presence of children in his ministry. As a matter of fact, children have always played an extremely important role in the faith community. Even in the Old Testament, many of the rituals and ceremonies focused on children in order to teach them about the faithfulness of their God. Jesus continues that theme. Children have real faith and have a real place within the faith community. Children are not just potential Christians, or believers-in-waiting. I truly believe that when a small child says, "I love Jesus," God rejoices as much at that statement of faith as he does with an adult confession.

Second, when Jesus used children as a model of faith, he wasn't suggesting that children somehow had all the answers or had penetrated all the mysteries of faith. Quite the contrary. I believe he was reminding adults that we had better be more trusting and more dependent on God the way young children naturally are. Children intuitively know they cannot function on their own; they need adults. Christians should intuitively know they cannot function on their own; they need God. Children also are much quicker to trust those close to them. At least in a healthy family situation, most children rarely question a parent's promise or commitment. Only when those commitments are not honored consistently does the child learn not to trust. So also, adults should have that same implicit trust that God will care for them. Having faith like a child helps an adult rest more easily in the arms of the Holy Father. You may find that your smaller children do become a model, in some ways, of accepting the death of your spouse more easily than you do. Try to learn from them.

Perhaps the best posture in dealing with the spiritual aspect of your children's grief is simply to encourage you to respect them. Listen carefully to them. Do not dismiss them or what they say. Regardless of how young or old they may be, your children are also on a journey to the other side of grief. You can walk that journey together.

Your children have *real fears* and *real faith*. Listen to both the fears and the expressions of faith. Perhaps one of the biggest fears, especially for small children, is that

you and God are also going to abandon them. It may
seem to them that one of their parents has already
abandoned them. Now is the time to reinforce for them
that God will never leave them, nor forsake them
(Deut. 31:8). But doing that in words isn't enough. Listen gently to their fears, and then God can work
through you to bring them some sense of peace and
wholeness again. Listen as well to their expressions of
faith. Often children can help a grieving parent cut
through some of the complexities of grief. How simple,
yet profound, is the seven-year-old daughter who hugs
her mother and says, "But I love you, Mommy, and God
does too."

Your children have *real questions* and *real answers.*
Their questions may not be shaped or formulated the
way yours might be, but their questions are still important. Just make certain you understand the question
first. Perhaps you know the story of six-year-old Matt
who asked his mother, "Where did I come from?" A little taken aback by the question, Matt's mother went
into a ten minute explanation of human reproduction
and birth. Finally she concluded, "You actually came
from inside me, Matt. But I'm curious, why do ask?"
"Oh," came Matt's reply, "Jamie just moved in next
door, and he said he came from Cincinnati."

So when your child asks, "What is heaven like?" ask
him or her first to answer their own question. "Well,
what do you think it's like, dear?" Then listen carefully.
All of the depictions of heaven recorded in the Bible
require the use of a vivid imagination, and in your
child's imagination, you may find another picture of
heaven you hadn't considered. Children can have good
answers, you know, and your child can probably teach
you a few things about how to use your imagination in
your grief.

Your children have *real hurts* and *real hopes*. I use a videotape in a course on youth culture that begins with a couple's reaction to the suicide of their oldest son. One thing they immediately do is force their high school senior to "just go to school" because he has to take exams. "We'll take care of this," the dialog goes, "you just do what you have to." Perhaps the scenario is exaggerated, but the point is well taken. Adults can quickly assume that children do not really hurt. Watch what happens in a funeral home when children are around. How many people really talk with them? How many people spend time with them later to help them work through their grief? Typically we tend to focus on the adult survivors or try to attend to the children's needs by talking about those needs with the adults rather than with the children directly.

Fortunately younger children can be very resilient spiritually. Their simple faith can carry them through. Faith involves a lot of mystery and a lot of trust. We do not have the answers, but our children really don't expect complete explanations. They simply want to know and see that their simple faith is still well-founded. They want to know that you still believe as well. They are not looking for solutions; they are looking for models. Walk with them on their journey to the other side of grief.

8

What about Financial and Employment Issues?
Traveling Back to Financial Reality

Stop the world. I want to get off!" How often have you felt like that since your spouse has died? You want the world to stop. Sometimes the pressure of all the decisions you have to make piles up to the point that you think you are going to snap. Even as you move past the funeral and begin to rebuild your life, you have to make so many tough choices.

The problem is—the world doesn't stop. The world doesn't take notice that another person has died. The world isn't really affected by the fact that one less person is here to pay bills, mow the lawn, or take the kids to school. You are left on your own. Perhaps surrounded by some family and a few close friends, you have to fend for yourself. And reality begins to sink in. Bills keep coming; the mortgage is due; and the family budget is in an upheaval.

Grief isn't limited merely to dealing with emotional feelings in quiet moments. The grieving process also involves hard, cold facts about money, employment, and housing. We hope you will read this chapter early in your grief because many survivors are tempted to make decisions about these important areas prematurely. We'd like to give you the confidence to manage them in the short term. Later, you can make more permanent decisions about these critical areas of your new life.

The Psychologist Says

It is never too late to be what you might have been.

George Eliot

Money Matters

We all need money, but finances are usually the last thing you want to think about when you have to deal with your grief. We all sense that a spouse's death is bad timing, especially if he or she died before reaching retirement age, and part of that bad timing is related to all the mundane decisions you now have to make. Older couples usually have made financial and housing plans in connection with their retirement. They tend to realize that they will die, and so they make some provision to cover each other's practical needs in case of the spouse's death. Finances are a little more stable after retirement because pensions, annuities, and social security are in place. They are not dependent on their spouse's actual employment income.

When a younger spouse dies, however, the loss of that income is an entirely different matter. Younger couples usually haven't planned for death—at least not in terms of some basic financial and housing decisions. Money is necessary for our survival, and most of us find that our current income is just enough to pay the mortgage, monthly bills, and other expenses. Many families have become dependent on a double income, and the financial demands do not stop when a spouse dies. Of course, the sting of the financial loss may be lessened if your spouse had some life insurance. In that case the money crisis may be eased somewhat, but that money may not be immediately available, especially if the will needs to be probated. You may also prefer to invest the life insurance money for future financial security rather than using it for daily living expenses.

So what can you and your family do to face the financial crisis that a death may cause? First of all, you need to find some way to manage the immediate future. You will undoubtedly feel the pressure to either lower your monthly expenses or find some other source of income. But if your spouse just died, you really are not at an optimum point to make such decisions. You would like to put it off for awhile. But bill collectors usually do not give much leeway, if any, in your monthly payments. Some widowed persons, therefore, are forced to make some short-term decisions that may not be in the best long-term interest of the surviving spouse or family. One temptation is to quickly sell your house and move to a smaller, less expensive home. Another temptation is to plunge full force into a job. Neither of these options, however, are ideal, and if possible you should keep these only as a last resort. From a psychological perspective, if at all possible, maintaining your current lifestyle and residence for the first year is the best. Remember that your present situation is not going to stay this way for the rest of your life.

Although we are not dealing with the financial issues for widows (women) only, in reality women face more financial crises than do men. Men tend to work full time and at higher paying jobs than do women. More often women work part time and are more involved with home and child-care responsibilities. Even if a woman works full time, she is often paid less than a man in a comparable position. Therefore, when a man dies, the survivor often suffers a major financial loss. Of course, if the traditional roles have been reversed, a man may find himself equally disadvantaged because of the loss of his wife's income. The man may also face another major challenge in that our culture still views the man as the primary financial provider. People may then tend to be less sensitive or aware of a man's financial crisis.

We suggest you use the following list as a point of reference to evaluate your own financial situation:

Helpful Suggestions

1. Check to see if you can consolidate bills so you have only one loan to pay off. You may be able to reduce your monthly payments and possibly your interest rate.
2. Investigate a second mortgage on your house, or try to increase the time period for paying off your current mortgage so you can have a better cash flow and smaller monthly payments.
3. Consult with a financial planner and investigate specific options before making

any major decisions about selling or moving. This is especially important if you have received a life insurance settlement.

4. Consider allowing family or close friends to help you financially for a short period of time until you can investigate your own options. Beware, however, of any implied obligations that may be attached to gifts or loans.

5. Most cities have some form of Displaced Homemaker Service or other assistance for people who no longer have a spouse and are forced to find a job to support themselves and their children. Check available resources for job training or job placement. Usually these services are provided at no cost.

6. Before entering the workforce or increasing your hours at work, carefully consider your emotional readiness for this move. Is it absolutely necessary? How long should you stay at home, especially if children are involved? Remember, in the long run spending more time at home may be in your best interest and that of your family. Even if you have no children at home, you will help your own grieving process by providing some time alone before plunging back into the workforce.

7. Your spouse may have had a pension or retirement plan for which you are eligible. Check into your benefits as a surviving spouse. At age sixty you can receive 71.5 percent of your deceased partner's social security benefits if you are not already re-

ceiving your own. Actually, you can receive either your own or your spouse's, whichever is higher. At age sixty-five you are entitled to 100 percent of either your own or your deceased partner's social security benefits, whichever is larger.

Going to Work

Most studies clearly indicate that you should not make major decisions too quickly after your spouse's death.[1] As we've said before, the tendency for you as the surviving spouse is to think that the way you feel today is the way you will feel for the rest of your life. This is definitely not true. If you cannot wait to get a job because of the financial pressures, at least go back to work with the attitude that this is temporary. Look at it as a way to make ends meet or get your feet wet before making a major decision. Sometimes widowed people think they have to make permanent decisions right away about what they will do for the rest of their life. But serious decisions should be delayed if at all possible because grieving itself is so encompassing that your mind simply cannot focus on these issues in a balanced way. We don't make the healthiest decisions unless we have full cognitive and emotional functioning in balance, and early in grief people tend to respond emotionally to most things. So we recommend that you make a temporary decision about a job that will meet your immediate financial needs, and wait at least one year to make a long-term choice. That doesn't guarantee you will be ready then, but in the meantime you need to work hard at assessing your own strengths and weaknesses as well as your likes and dislikes and setting your own personal goals in the context of job preferences and personal capabilities.

You may also decide that you now have an opportunity to pursue an education or a career you hadn't been able to consider before. Many times couples make joint decisions about employment that complement their relationship, but those choices do not necessarily reflect your own personal preferences now that you are single. One of the advantages of being single is that you now can, and have to, make your decisions without considering someone else's needs or desires. Of course this may sound a little harsh, especially if your spouse just died. We do not mean to minimize all the disadvantages you now face. However, one central clue that indicates you are ready to make more responsible decisions is when you are able to look at the positive side of a situation that had initially been overwhelmingly negative. When you are ready to do this, you have made major strides in the process of grieving.

Where to Live?

Some survivors find they simply cannot continue to live in their present residence when their spouse dies. Maybe you just can't meet the mortgage payments, or there could be other factors in your personal life that simply make it impossible to stay where you are. As we have said before, really test this decision to move. Are there really no other short-term options? Adding the stress of a move on top of the stress of your grief is very difficult. Grieving, as you may already know, is an exhausting process. So is moving. To do both at the same time is virtually impossible, so in most cases the grieving would be pushed to the background. If you have children, their lives have also been disrupted by their parent's death, and they don't need any more stress. It is important to maintain stability for the children by remaining in their same home, school system, and in contact with their friends if at all possible. You have probably already established some support systems where you live now, and you are familiar with the makeup of your local community—shopping, schools, recreation, churches, etc. Changing all that can be stressful.

You may have some pressure from well-meaning family and friends about what they think is best for you. Your extended family may want you to move closer to them so they can help. Possibly they think your home is too large and unmanageable for you. Try to resist their pressure; you need to make this decision for yourself and your children. While their advice may be helpful, ultimately you are the one who has to decide. Take plenty of time to consider some of the important factors in making a decision about housing. For example, housing costs should not exceed 30 percent of your income. Decisions about housing also need to be made in light of social needs, educational considerations, spiritual components, and work location.

If there is no reasonable way to remain in your present location, then you need to make a major adjustment in your grieving process. Instead of shelving your grief, look at the move to another residence as an opportunity to bring a form of physical closure—a way of saying good-bye to your grief. Touching, packing, and moving your favorite things will likely trigger many memories. You can use this opportunity in a healthy way if you allow yourself time to relish those memories, store them in a new place in your heart, and then put them behind you. But this will be healthy only when a person is ready to move on. If you try to do it too quickly, you may have an extremely difficult time emotionally.

If you do have to move and you have children at home, involve them to some degree in the moving process. Invite them to help you sort through things, pack them in boxes, and dream about new room arrangements in your new place. Try very hard to include them, since they also have lost a significant person in their lives. You are now their only surviving parent. Be sensitive to the fact that this is undoubtedly hard for all of you.

On the other hand, the children do not have to be involved in every single aspect of the move. Consider asking a family member or friend to take the children to lunch or a movie once in a while. This will give you some private time to sort through your collection of personal memorabilia. Perhaps you and your spouse had collected special pictures, trinkets from trips, or other mementos that remind you of your special relationship. We encourage you to use this time for some catharsis. Vent your emotions; cry; remember; savor the memories. Doing this will help you move on in your journey rather than postponing this emotional release. Your emotions will surface later if you don't deal with them now.

A Year or More Later

If you are at a point where you no longer feel intense pain over the loss of your spouse and you are somewhat comfortable looking at your life now with a renewed energy to evaluate and make decisions, then you are probably ready to face the issues of employment and housing for the long term. Originally, you probably selected a job or a residence to meet your needs as a married couple. Those needs were important at the time, but your personal needs have probably changed. Instead of making blended choices involving two of you, you now have the opportunity to explore what you alone think, feel, want, and need with respect to your home and job. You are now free to examine yourself, identify your options, and decide your own course toward the future. This can be a very exciting, though scary, time in your life. Remember that positive choices can be as stressful and as anxiety producing as some negative situations, but rather than representing negative stresses or distress, they represent something new and adventuresome. Have the courage to face what comes next.

The Pastor Says

I will do whatever you ask in my name.

John 14:13

No one whose hope is in you will ever be put to shame.

Psalm 25:3

God the Provider

Partners in a marriage provide so much for each other. They provide companionship, encouragement, and intimacy. They share dreams and ambitions, and they begin to blend their lives so much that they often speak of *our* hopes and dreams, and then they work together in pursuit of those dreams. More frequently both partners have a job, and they share their income. All expenses are paid out of a common pot as they build their estate.

In the process, two things can happen—one psychological and the other spiritual. The psychological result is that each person begins to depend on the other, sometimes to the point that their personal identity becomes extremely entangled with the other person. For example, neither has his or her personal money—especially the wife if it is a traditional marriage relationship. Neither has much personal time or friends alone. Lives have been blended, and a certain level of comfort settles in because they each begin to rely on the other to provide for their mutual needs.

The spiritual consequence is that often couples begin to look to each other rather than to God for those daily, earthly provisions. After all, they need to budget, plan, work, and spend. Couples make their decisions together in keeping with what each one can contribute—what each one can provide for this joint effort. In the process, they may be tempted to lose sight of the fact that God is the provider.

When your spouse dies, the issue of providing for your life meets you head-on. Typically, pastors and church members say they will pray for you. Usually, that means they will pray that you will be able to find peace in your heart, reach a point of acceptance of the death, cope with the stresses of adjusting to your new single status, and (perhaps) handle some of the other emotional side effects. If you are a widow, perhaps a deacon may ask a general question like, "How are you getting along?"—trying to hint at some financial concerns. If you are a man, that might not even happen.

When my wife died, she was earning a full income from her career as a teacher. Even during her illness, she was receiving disability income. Even though I was well established in my career with a stable salary, one of my earliest and biggest concerns following her death was how I was going to manage financially. My youngest daughter was still in college, I anticipated other major expenses (my children were all getting near the age of marriage), and our family income was now cut nearly in half. Yet no one asked. No one seemed to think finances would be an issue for me. I had to wrestle with how God was going to be a provider.

That God does provide is beyond question. The Bible is filled with examples of how God provides for those in need, such as:

- *Manna and quail in the desert in Exodus 16.* God provided for the Israelites while they wandered in the wilderness for forty years. Every day they received their food directly from the hand of God. As a matter of fact, their clothes never even wore out (Deut. 8:4).
- *The widow's oil in 2 Kings 4:1–7.* God worked a miracle so the widow could not only feed Elisha, the prophet, but her little jar of oil suddenly filled all the jars in her house. She had enough oil to sell the excess and pay her debts.
- *Wine at the wedding in John 2:1–11.* Jesus was not concerned only about people in desperate situations or under the threat of starvation; he also wanted a wedding to go well. He wanted people to celebrate and enjoy this momentous occasion. When the wine ran out, Jesus miraculously took six stone jars filled with water and converted them into the best wine of the night.
- *A boy's bread and fish in John 6:5–13.* Jesus took a boy's small lunch of bread and fish to feed a gathering of five thousand people. The amazing thing is that the scraps filled twelve baskets—leftovers that far exceeded the boy's original lunch.

The examples of God's provision could continue almost endlessly, and many of them are miracles. Maybe you don't think God can or wants to do a miracle for you. But the point is that God is the provider, and he will take care of those in need if they ask in faith.

How does that work? If that is true, why are we not all rich? Why are we not all well cared for? Why do some of us face financial ruin? Should we all join "The Church of Abundant Life," which sent me a promotional mailing a number of years ago? The cover of this poorly duplicated flyer depicted a sun whose rays were filled with cars, television sets, boats, dollar bills, and all sorts of other material things. Under the picture were the words: "Ask and it will be given to you" (Matt. 7:7). What's wrong with that picture?

The lesson of the passages above is that we must reverse our priorities. While attending to our material needs is important, these things are not the most important. God, in essence, is saying, "Don't worry about the small stuff." And all of this is—to God—"small stuff." Just as God provided food for the Israelites in the wilderness *one day at a time* so they could continue their journey to the Promised Land, he will provide for your daily needs as you proceed on your journey.

In my own grief journey, I had to face several hard decisions that affected finances, housing, and jobs. In the first three years after Char died, I had seriously considered at least four concrete career or job offers, made a number of decisions about life insurance proceeds, significantly reorganized my finances, watched all three children get married, and sold my house. None of these decisions or experiences were easy. They all took a great deal of emotional energy, a lot of talking with close friends, much time in prayer, and a real desire to follow God's lead. I'm not sure I always made the right decisions—especially the ones I made early in my grief process. But God provides!

Needs versus Wants

You may need to learn to reevaluate or redefine needs and wants. I am amazed how quickly and subtly my wants become my needs. It happens frequently. Somehow an idea gets planted in the brain, it takes root, a desire begins to emerge, and soon I have a new need. And I'm talking about simple things: a new golf club, computer printer, pair of shoes, television set, or CD player.

God has a way of redefining wants and needs. In teaching us to pray for "our daily bread" in the Lord's Prayer (Matt. 6:11), he is really instructing us to rely on him daily for our needs. This is a time to examine your lifestyle. As you rebuild your life, what do you really need? The list of needs may be very short and very general. You need housing; you need an income; you need friends; but most of all you need God. You may want a certain type of housing, a certain level of income, a certain group of friends—but here is where you need to find a delicate balance between pursuing your wants while accepting the fact that God may lead you in a different, and usually more exciting, direction.

I really didn't know how my financial life would come back together again. I don't think, however, that I had a naive faith when I simply clung to verses like, "In all things God works for the good of those who love him" (Rom. 8:28). I knew I still needed to plan and make responsible decisions.

I had mentioned in an earlier chapter that the simple verse of Jesus from the Sermon on the Mount became my life verse: "But seek first his kingdom and his righteousness, and all these things will be given to you as well" (Matt. 6:33). The apostle Paul once wrote, "I have learned the secret of being content in any and every situation, . . . whether living in plenty or in want" (Phil. 4:12). And what was his secret? "I can do everything through him who gives me strength" (Phil. 4:13). By redefining most of your needs back into wants, you open the door for this open-ended type of faith that relies on God to provide daily for all your needs.

Receive without Expecting

Some time ago a silly little story was making the circuit about a couple stranded on top of their house in a torrent of rising flood water. As the water continued to rise, several people came by to rescue them. First a man came in a canoe, then someone in a speedboat, and finally, just as the water was beginning to crest over the roof line, a helicopter came. Each time, the couple refused their offers of help. "We're Christians, and we're praying that God will save us." They drowned, and when they appeared at the pearly gates they confronted the Lord: "Why didn't you save us! We were praying all the time, and we believed you would come to our rescue." The Lord's response was, "I tried three times, and you refused." Silly story. But maybe not quite as silly as we may think.

How often do we pray *solutions* rather than requests? How often do we tell God how to fix the problem rather than allowing God to provide his own solution? If you are a Christian, you undoubtedly prayed that God would heal your spouse. You undoubtedly clung to promises that God would hear your prayers. But now it may seem to you that God didn't agree with your solution. Trying to understand why bad things happen to good people is very difficult. Somehow you have to balance two seemingly opposing thoughts—that God can do anything he wants and that bad things still happen.

Somehow we have to learn to accept the fact that God allows some of these bad things to happen even though he doesn't want them to anymore than you do. But you also need to know that he can take all those situations and, in his own way and time, turn them to your benefit.

Jesus himself serves as the model. While in the Garden of Gethsemane, Jesus knew he was destined to go to the cross, yet he still let his Father know what he wanted. Anticipating the agony and pain, he prayed, "My Father, if it is possible, may this cup be taken from me" (Matt. 26:39). He let God know what he wanted, but he immediately added the words, "Yet not as I will, but as you will."

Praying that God's will be done is not a cop-out. When prayed in the right attitude, you are committing an act of faith that our gracious God will be the provider. Once you yield to him on that point, be as free as Jesus himself in letting God know what you would want—confident that God will provide.

Stewardship of Your Life

Be a good steward of all your life regardless of the circumstances. When you are grieving, you may tend to become very self-focused. In many ways this self-focus is healthy and good. Some people promote the acronym J.O.Y.—Jesus is first, Others are second, and You are third. This approach is extremely simplistic and does *not* represent Scripture's teaching. The relationship between Christ, others, and you is not sequential. You must attend purposefully to each of these three areas. We certainly hear a lot of Christian messages instructing us to put Christ first and others second. The implication is that you must negate yourself or pay less attention to your needs in this process. That conclusion is false. You deserve and need to pay attention to yourself. You need time to figure out your own needs, strategies, and goals for your newly emerging life.

Spiritually, however, this self-focus ultimately needs to be kept in balance. I often use the word *stewardship* for this phenomenon, but I quickly want to add that I am not talking about stewardship in the narrow, financial sense of the word. I am speaking about using all your resources, gifts, talents, and experiences in service of God's kingdom. The bottom line is summarized best in saying that by giving, you receive. I am impressed with Paul's words in 2 Corinthians 1:3–4.

> Praise be to the God and Father of our Lord Jesus Christ, the Father of compassion and the God of all comfort, who comforts us in all our troubles, so that we can comfort those in any trouble with the comfort we ourselves have received from God.

I began to experience the first part of that verse— that God is a God of "all comfort" and that he will comfort us. What really struck me, however, was the phrase "so that. . . ." Being comforted by God has a purpose beyond myself—I am to be a steward of my comfort. I wish now that I had seen that earlier. Rather than trying to keep my grief inside, rather than trying to handle it by myself, I now believe that if I had sought out other hurting people we would have been far better equipped to comfort each other. I know that is a strange definition of stewardship, but I want to encourage you not to hoard your grief. Share it with others when you feel ready because in the sharing you will not only comfort others, but you will find comfort yourself.

This principle applies to all the aspects of your life. Try to return to your usual service involvements when you have worked through your own grief. Did you volunteer somewhere before your spouse died? Start doing that again—at least for a while until you decide whether this type of involvement is still most meaningful for you. Focusing on others' needs in balance with your own is a productive way for you to put your own situation into a healthy context.

Waiting On the Lord

Waiting is one of the hardest things for me to do. But God tells us time and again to wait on him. "They that wait upon the Lord shall renew their strength" (Isa. 40:31 KJV). God provides, but in his own time. Growing together as husband and wife took a long time. Don't expect to unweave your life tapestry overnight. We live in a culture that expects nearly instant gratification; everything needs to be "hot and now." Grieving doesn't work that way, nor do major financial decisions. Allow yourself the luxury of time. Remind yourself that taking your time is, in fact, not a luxury but a necessity.

Spend time alone with yourself and with God. If your religious tradition encourages the use of spiritual directors, find one to walk with you on your journey. Use spiritual retreat houses to take a time out from all the pressures and stresses. Learn the art of meditation. Set aside a specific time each day to sit and think, meditate, or listen to your favorite hymns or choruses.

You already know there are no quick and easy answers. Grieving takes time, and grieving requires a lot of energy. Your situation will not change overnight, but it will change. God not only provides solutions, he provides strength as you wait and work toward those solutions.

9

What Is the Other Side of Grief?

Completing the Journey and Moving On

Do you remember what it's like to be stuck in a traffic jam? Minutes drag on like hours. Your car creeps at a snail's pace. Other drivers vent their frustration by trying to sneak past on the shoulder. Truckers linger back, creating huge gaps in the traffic. If only you could get around them! If only you could get to the other side of the mess. And you finally do. You move past the roadblock and spring down the highway free of obstructions, rapidly leaving the frustration behind. You've gotten to the other side.

Grieving has another side. Every ending contains within itself the seeds of a new beginning. Throughout this book we have taken the position that grief is a temporary condition that can be resolved. Grief does not have to hold you in its grip; you can move through it. We have also held the position, however, that you must take an active role in moving through that grief. You can't just park along the shoulder and expect the traffic to disappear. If you want healing to happen, you must take charge and consciously begin to build a new life for yourself. That life will certainly be different from your life prior to your spouse's death. But different is not bad. We hope that as you read and reread this book, you will come to the point to which this chapter leads you—moving on to the other side of grief.

The Psychologist Says

I can dream of the old days,
Life was beautiful then.
I remember a time I knew what happiness was,
Let the memories live again. . . .

I must think of a new life
And I mustn't give in,
When the dawn comes,
Tonight will be a memory too.
              "Memories," from the musical *Cats*

Memories and Moving On

Memories. Beautiful, wonderful memories. They will remain, but the actual past cannot. To move on and begin a new volume in your life does not mean you have to forget the one you loved. Your spouse was a part of your life—just as your childhood, adolescence, and young adulthood were a part of your life and now are part of your memories. But you haven't stayed there; you have moved along in your life. Your life with your spouse in the past helped define who and what you are, and those memories will not disappear or be erased. But those memories cannot help you live in the present. Do not let them overshadow the joys that can come right now. You can retain those parts of yourself that grew and developed with your deceased spouse, and now you can close that marriage volume of your life and begin another new and exciting volume.

One can't move on while holding on. That means that in order to start taking some steps forward in your life, you have to release your grasp on the past. Moving on may be very difficult if you continue to try to keep one foot planted in the past while the other foot edges toward the future. The process of letting go and moving on means that eventually the present will no longer seem gloomy and dismal. You have reached a monumental point in your journey when you realize you can go on alone—solo—as a single person. And you will know you are even farther down the road when you begin to look forward to what you might do next rather than continuing to grieve over what cannot be changed in the past. The grieving process is a way of healing your broken heart in order to become whole again. If you don't find yourself there yet, don't give up. That time will come if you continue to work on your grief and overcome the necessary hurdles.

You are ready to move forward when you recognize that the intense pain is gone and you can bring a tentative closure to that prior volume of your life. We intentionally use the word *volume* to represent a significant time period and relationship with your deceased spouse. But like the first volume of a major journalistic work, that portion is now complete, bound, and on the shelf. Your own life continues; you are beginning a new volume. That means you stop and acknowledge that you have worked through the pain of losing your spouse.

This is a significant accomplishment! Give yourself credit for having faced and dealt with the difficult realities of the grief journey. Name and summarize the significant milestones you have passed during the process of your grieving. Relate the experience of your loss to your new context. Write down the story of your grief. Do something special to signify the closure of this volume in your life and the opening of a new one. Recognize that there may be a mixture of excitement and apprehension; it is natural to have some anxiety about beginning a new phase in your life. But you have an opportunity to begin again—to move on.

> And you learn to build all your roads
> On today because tomorrow's ground
> Is too uncertain. And futures have
> A way of falling down in midflight.
>
> And you learn that you really can endure . . .
> That you really are strong
> And you really do have worth
> And you learn and learn . . .
> With every good-bye you learn.[1]

HELPFUL SUGGESTIONS

1. Assess your emotional level. Are you still functioning in pain from the loss of your deceased spouse? If you still experience waves of anguished grief (crying and feeling depressed), wait before moving on to your next life phase. Return to previous chapters to revisit applicable assignments for grieving. It would be unfair to yourself and to a potential partner to leave your past volume unfinished before moving on.

Settling for only partial work in both your old and new volumes will detract from both.

2. Make certain you have developed some way to hold pleasant memories in your mind through picture albums, journaling stories, or collected mementos that can highlight your past marriage.

3. If you believe you are able to close the volume on your past marriage, pause and give yourself credit for the hard work you have done and for all the hurdles you have jumped. Celebrate your accomplishment, and reread your journal. Summarize your journal by writing a reflective view of your grief journey to explain and signify closure of that volume of your life.

4. Go on an overnight or weekend trip by yourself to concretely signify the end of grieving and the beginning of a new life phase.

Is There Old Baggage?

When you are ready to move on, ask yourself if you are carrying any old baggage. If you are aware of any unresolved issues, now is a good time to deal with them. By unresolved issues we mean that there may have been some unreconciled element in your relationship, or something had occurred that you have not looked at, or someone else has died or left and you haven't dealt with the situation. As you start a new phase in your life, you don't want to burden yourself with unnecessary past issues.

How do you know when you are through grieving? You will know that you have completed the majority of your grieving when:

- Thoughts of your deceased spouse are no longer depressing or painful—only a sweet sadness remains with memories that are now largely pleasant and wonderful.
- You enjoy life again and can celebrate holidays and other significant events with an eager anticipation of trying new things and making plans for the future.
- Your level of functioning in all areas is at least comparable to your prebereavement level.
- You have developed some form of rational explanation for your spouse's death, even if it is simply that death is part of life, versus continuing to ask yourself, "Why me?"
- You are able to cope with other losses (i.e., having enough energy to face other difficult circumstances such as funerals), and you are able to support others with their losses.

If you do not think you are through your grief yet, do not despair. Consider what you may need to revisit and then deal with it. Perhaps you might reread those sections of this book that deal with your continuing issues. Repeat some of the suggestions. Talk with other widowed persons or consider seeing a therapist who does grief counseling.

HELPFUL SUGGESTIONS

1. Assess specific aspects of your relationship with your deceased spouse one more time.

Are you still carrying any baggage or remembering situations about which you would rather not think? Eventually it will be harmful to keep putting it out of your mind. Take the time to reframe your thinking of that difficulty or problem so that you are kind to yourself. Undoubtedly if your partner were still alive, you would have arrived at some resolution. So now do that for yourself.

2. Besides clearing your thoughts, clear your living space of that old baggage as well. Allow no shrines to the past. Be careful not to idealize your spouse. Your mate was human like the rest of us and made mistakes too, so don't place that person on a pedestal. Sometimes this takes the form of clinging to artifacts from the deceased and displaying them in a manner inconsistent with moving on. Old baggage is hard to live with, perhaps difficult to give up, but holding onto it is unhealthy.

Wedding Rings and Pictures

As you move toward a new chapter in your life, you will need to address both the matter of wearing your wedding ring and what you will do about pictures of your deceased spouse in your home. These two items are powerful symbols of a time gone by—a valued sign of the memories of your former marriage and the previous volume of your life.

There is no right time to remove your wedding ring, but if you are planning to move on toward a new phase in your life, you will need to decide if you want

to wear the ring on another finger or remove it alto-
gether. In our culture, wearing the ring on the fourth
finger of your left hand symbolizes that the wearer is
married or in a committed relationship. When a person does not wear a ring on that finger, other people
simply know that the wearer is not married or in a serious relationship. The empty finger does not mean
you are necessarily looking for another relationship;
it simply means you are not married. And the reality
for you as a widowed person is that you are now not
married. You may have wonderful memories of that
time in your life, but the fact remains that you no
longer have that relationship. Helping yourself face
that reality and seeing yourself as a single person is a
healthy accomplishment.

You may have removed your wedding ring some time
ago. When my husband died, I knew I could no longer
wear my wedding ring because he was no longer here
to carry on a relationship with me. Somehow wearing
the ring seemed to me unaccepting of the reality of his
death. So I took the ring off, had the diamonds from
both his and my ring reset, and during the time prior
to my remarriage I wore the new ring on my right hand.
Moving the ring from my left hand in no way signified
that I was looking for another relationship. On the contrary, the removal of the ring was an act of facing the
reality that I was no longer married. Having the diamonds reset into a new ring allowed me to symbolize
in a new way that special and valued volume in my life.
You have many healthy options to choose from in deciding what to do with your wedding ring. Besides having the ring reset, you could place the stone in another
piece of jewelry (e.g., a necklace or pin), keep it until
an adult child marries, save it for some other significant occasion to pass it on to an heir, or keep it in a

safety deposit box until you decide what you would like to do with it. Make a choice that suits you best.

Displaying pictures of your deceased spouse around your home is a traditional way to remember happy, joyful occasions shared with your former partner. You may have accumulated many pictures of you as a couple or as a family. After Rick died, I found comfort in having his pictures around me even though they sometimes triggered tears because I missed him so much. Two and a half years after his death, I recognized just how many pictures I did have on display, and I also recognized that I no longer needed those pictures to comfort me. My life has been redefined. I needed to decide which pictures I still wanted to keep on display and which to put away. I also needed to decide where I might want to display them. I wanted to make room for new pictures that symbolize the joy of moving on to the next volume of my life.

Perhaps you are at the point where you want to assess your attachment to pictures of your spouse and determine what role they serve. You may decide that the pictures might interfere with the next phase of your single life. Removing them may be difficult. Change is difficult, but change can also be invigorating and exciting.

HELPFUL SUGGESTIONS

1. If you have not made a decision about removing your wedding ring from the fourth finger of your left hand, now may be an appropriate time to do so. The wedding ring is a symbol of a marriage—a union and commitment between two living persons. That commitment ended with the death of your spouse. Removal of your ring as that

> symbol is a mark of a healthy transition toward moving on.
> 2. Assess how many pictures of your deceased spouse you have around the house. Evaluate how many photos you want to keep out and where in your house you wish to display them. Try to keep these photos proportionate to the past, especially to make room for the future.

Figuring Yourself Out

Figuring out who you really are now is an interesting endeavor. How do you answer the questions:

- Who am I by myself?
- Where am I right now?
- Where do I want to be?
- What do I want for myself out of life?

If you knew the answers to those questions before your spouse died, that will be of some help now. But as you well know, your life is very different now, so these questions must be asked again. If you never really asked yourself those questions before, this will be an especially challenging—but hopefully exciting—endeavor.

If you allowed your previous marriage relationship to primarily define who you were and what you wanted, you have the challenge of figuring out who you really are now and what you want to be. You will certainly be able to build on the past because it is an integral part of you. You will need to engage in a lot of introspection to ask what will make you happy, what were your dreams for yourself before and during your marriage, and what are they now. You will want to reassess what life values are important to you. At times it may seem as though your life is being demolished rather than being rebuilt, but slowly you will add pieces to the project and your new image will emerge.

All this is a process of becoming totally "you" again— to know what you want apart from your deceased spouse. In this way you will be better prepared to move on toward the future. Slowly you will discover how capable you really are as you venture out to try new things on your own, becoming more independent as you stretch yourself. Encourage yourself with words of reaffirmation. Simply remind yourself (even say outloud): "I am a widowed person; I am single; I am okay by myself; I am a good person; I have a future."

Now the future is yours; it belongs to you and you alone. You could decide to merely exist and allow yourself to get stuck in the grief process, but why spend your life mourning and being miserable over something you cannot change? Embrace the message: "Don't die until you are dead." The death of a spouse is a very hard way to learn something about the essence of life, but learning about life's fragility and brevity can also enrich your life. You can learn again to make the most of the time God gives you on this earth. God put you here for various reasons, and those reasons did not end when your spouse died. Find out what those reasons are. Write a new verse to the poem of your life by living your life to the fullest as you continue your journey to the other side of grief.

HELPFUL SUGGESTIONS

1. Be able to verbalize or list five to ten of your positive characteristics or strengths. Conversely, be able to identify your weaknesses

or vulnerabilities. Get to know yourself as
you are right now so you can continue to
develop even more fully and become all
that you can be.
2. Identify some interests, activities, or hob-
bies you enjoy or would like to explore to
confirm who you are as an individual.

To Remain Single or to Remarry

We briefly discussed the issue of remaining single or
remarrying in chapter 5 in the sections "Meeting Your
Sexual Needs" and "Heterosexual Friendships, Dating,
and Remarriage." You may wish to refer to those sections if you are reading this chapter some time later.

We want to be very clear that there is no preferred
or right way to continue your life as a surviving spouse.
There are advantages and disadvantages to both remaining single and to remarrying. If you have been widowed for one to three years and have gone through most
of your grief, you may now be on the other side enjoying your freedom and independence. You now have the
freedom to make your own decisions without having to
accommodate or compromise.

You may have experienced yourself as much more
capable and competent than you previously thought
possible. You may have taken on the challenge of
being single and have successfully done things by and
for yourself. That can feel great! Not to have to consider what a partner wants or needs before doing what
you are inclined to do is a freeing experience. Now
you can do exactly what you want to do about financial matters or dealing with children, friends, and family. For some surviving spouses, this can be exciting
and liberating.

For others, however, this may have a serious negative side. To have to do all the decision making and to retain all the responsibility may at times feel burdensome and lonely. Having someone in your life to share these tasks and decisions may appeal to you. Having someone to talk with and to share both small and big things can be both comforting and exhilarating.

Wouldn't it be wonderful if our choices could simply be between completely positive or negative options? This would make decision making easy. We would only have to choose those options that have purely positive consequences. Unfortunately, adult choices usually have both pros and cons associated with them. They are a mixture of both positive and negative, and each of us must sort through those choices for ourselves. This is strictly an individual matter based on each person's own thoughts, feelings, wants, and needs. You will need to engage in a lot of soul-searching, self-assessment, and prayer to determine what is the best course for you.

HELPFUL SUGGESTION

Evaluate your level of satisfaction in remaining a single person versus the pros and cons of dating and perhaps moving toward remarriage. It may be that while writing out the pros and cons of each choice and rating their importance (on a scale of 1 to 5, with 5 being the highest), you will see more clearly a healthy solution.

The Choice to Stay Single

As a surviving spouse, you are now single. If you don't do anything about that situation, you will remain single. And perhaps you are at a point in your life where you truly do not want to combine your life with another person's life in an intimate emotional and physical relationship. To be married once was enough. Maybe your marriage was a very positive experience, and now you simply don't want to do it again. Perhaps your marriage was a good marriage, but you are too weary of the caretaking and compromise that is involved in a good marriage, and you don't want to take the risks involved in committing again to another relationship. On the other hand, perhaps your previous marriage was not a happy experience and you simply don't want to repeat it. Maybe you are burned out and exhausted, and you now want to focus on your own life again.

Not every widowed person wants to remarry. As a matter of fact, many widowed persons never remarry—especially females. Some do not remarry because that is their personal preference. Others do not remarry because, for women, there generally are not enough men available for a new relationship. Some widowed persons may not want to learn to live with another person, and they may choose to have a few (or even one) close friendships that do not result in marriage.

Fortunately, the '90s is a time when you have acceptable alternatives to marriage if you decide you want to remain single. You may want to enjoy your independence and mobility. Or remaining single may be a temporary decision, leaving open the option that later on you might meet someone with whom you would like to partner. Hopefully our society has progressed to the point that individual decisions can be honored. The issue of remarriage or remaining single is strictly your own choice. Social pressures or expectations should play no role in your decision-making process.

HELPFUL SUGGESTIONS

1. Reaffirm yourself as a single person. Your decision to remain single (at least for now) is a healthy choice. List the things you wish to do to grow and develop, and list specific ways through which you can pursue them.
2. Appreciate the advantages of singleness and celebrate them. Evaluate the type of relationships you have so that your affiliation needs are met even though you choose not to be in an exclusive, committed relationship. Make certain you have opportunities to form friendships that enrich your life and assuage your loneliness. You will need to decide on the appropriate number of friendships and associations that work for you.

Is It Really a Choice to Remarry?

Some widowed persons may want to remarry but are not able to find a person with whom they feel comfortable and compatible as a future spouse. This can be very frustrating and difficult. To know that you desire to be in an intimate relationship with someone, but then not being able to fulfill that desire is tough. There is not a lot you can do in a situation like that.

The healthiest course is to continue to pursue your own interests and goals. Focus on being yourself, doing the things you like. In doing this, you may ultimately meet someone else who shares those interests and goals. If not, you are still enjoying your life for the most part. You have probably discovered by now that God doesn't always work according to our sense of timing. Take comfort in the fact that God holds your future in his hand, and ultimately he will work things out in your life—but on his time, not necessarily yours. Trust God, and be certain that he will take care of you and be there for you even if you are uncertain about how he will accomplish that. Tomorrow may be the day you will meet that special person who will enhance your life.

Helpful Suggestions

1. Remind yourself that the possibility of remarrying in a healthy way is quite uncertain. Remarriage depends on finding an appropriate person to date. This may happen, but you just don't know when or where. Be assured that God knows with certainty what will happen, and trust in his ability to bring someone into your life at the right point in time.

2. Choosing to keep an open mind about finding a potential partner is a significant decision. Give yourself credit for doing a self-assessment and for determining what suits your personality and needs the best. Learn to be patient as you continue to live your life to the fullest.

What to Consider Regarding Remarriage

Getting married for a second time typically is much more complicated than the first time a person marries. Think back to the first time you walked down the aisle. You probably had no children. You likely had minimal financial assets, investments, or real estate, no existing set of in-laws, no established adult social patterns, and likely no rooted career with some longevity. You were

probably quite young and starting out with few accumulated functioning patterns or material possessions.
Life was probably quite simple and exciting, with few
obstacles. That is traditionally a typical experience for
the first time around. You now have added multiple factors and issues that need to be examined that did not
exist before.

Now that you have been widowed and are possibly
thinking about dating and remarriage, consider why you
want to remarry and examine if these are healthy reasons. Some of the reasons widowed persons have given
for remarriage are love, security, companionship, money,
and sex. Remember that remarriage does not mean re-
placement. When a person remarries impulsively or soon
after his or her spouse's death, it is often done to counter
loneliness, sexual frustration, or insecurity. These impulsive reasons are psychologically unhealthy because
they are based on intense but mostly reactive and temporary needs. Research shows that over half of remar-
riages within the first two years of widowhood end in
divorce.[2] Many of those dissolutions occurred because
people were reacting to their fears and needs rather than
deciding to add to or enhance their lives. It is extremely
important to be personally grounded and feel comfortable with yourself as a single person before you begin to
look for a potential marital partner.

Some healthy reasons to consider remarriage are because you both like and love this new person, your time
together is filled with laughter and enjoyable companionship, and you share a variety of interests and values.
Other reasons may be that your rhythm and pace of life
are similarly tuned, your physical and sexual desires and
expectations are synchronized, and you enjoy sharing
time and space with this person. This person does not
really complete you—you are already a complete per-

son. But this person complements and enhances you in such a way that you both find a unity even within your own individuality. Partnering with this new person is like ordering a steak and lobster combination for dinner. Each item stands alone as a complete entree; however, combining the two creates a new taste experience.

HELPFUL SUGGESTION

Write down your reasons for remarrying, and evaluate them for their healthiness and appropriateness. Make certain the reasons do not involve neediness, but rather that this person will make your life more special.

Dating the Second Time Around

If the thought of dating right now seems adulterous or sacrilegious, put it on hold for a while. Readiness to date is an extremely important factor, and being torn between your previous life and reaching toward a new one or feeling guilty about dating are signs that you should finish grieving before proceeding. One's desire to date again may also be affected by age. It seems that many people widowed in their seventies or later are not interested in remarriage. Persons in that age group may simply decide to enhance their life with good male and female friendships. Older women tend to outlive men in this age group, so there are fewer opportunities to meet available men as they get older.

To most people, going on a date again feels strange and somewhat adolescent. For many widowed persons, it has been some time since they went through that process. You may feel awkward and initially not as self-assured as usual. Know that these are all normal experiences.

Dating may have changed since you last did this. For instance, the sexes practice more equality in the '90s. Don't assume that the man picks the woman up for a date or pays the bill. In fact, a woman would be wise to drive herself and meet her date at a public place the first few times for safety's sake. In an ongoing dating relationship, taking turns driving may be something worth considering. Casual sex is also more common, so recognize that this might be an issue. Carefully consider and identify your own personal boundaries regarding sexual activity prior to getting involved with a dating partner. Examine your values and beliefs, and set firm guidelines based on your personal and religious values about the limits you will keep so you will not feel compromised. It is psychologically healthy not to rush into a physical relationship or to have the sexual side of a relationship develop prematurely prior to forming the deeper emotional ties of friendship and establishing reliable communication patterns. Determining the value, connectedness, and appropriateness of a relationship is more difficult when a physical relationship precedes the emergence of love and commitment.

Before you begin to date, considering what you really want in a potential partner is very healthy. Because you were previously married, you probably know more clearly what things are important or essential for you in a marriage partner. If you are dating with the intention of developing a long-term, committed relationship, make sure you have taken time to develop a clear description of what you want and do not want in a partner. Writing those things down is a good idea. Some of the various categories to consider when selecting a dating partner are:

- the person's previous relationship history
- the person's educational and work history

- the person's current job or career status
- geographical location—where this person lives
- religious beliefs and church preference
- financial status and practices
- lifestyle values and choices, including the use of alcohol and drugs
- medical history
- recreational interests
- style of socializing with friends
- family system including relationship with children, extended family, and previous in-laws
- the person's level of self-esteem
- the person's beliefs about equality and mutuality in a relationship
- the person's ability to communicate, compromise, and resolve conflicts

You can check on some of these factors very early—perhaps even before accepting a date. If you already know, based on your criteria, that no healthy marital relationship could develop, don't even go out the first time. Be in control of the process.

You do not have to get married again, but if you decide you want to find another partner, approach the matter deliberately. Begin to collect data early, within the first few times you go out, and be aware of how this person fits or does not fit your expectations and criteria. If there are any red flags that contradict your core values, beliefs, or philosophy of living, act as soon as you become aware of them and end the relationship. Avoid letting yourself say, "I'm just dating him or her; I'm not going to marry this person." Too many times widowed persons crave the attention and companionship of another so much that they may minimize their commitment to their own criteria.

This is the time to be as realistic and objective as possible. Remember that life will move on; there will be other people to date, and being with someone who is not well matched to your interests and standards is much more difficult and unhealthy than remaining single. There are many healthy people out there, but there are also people who had multiple problematic marriages, persons needing to be taken care of, persons who are presently married but dissatisfied with their current relationship, and substance abusers. This isn't meant to frighten you about this process, but it will be helpful to remember that dating later in life is different than the first time you dated.

The best way to know if the person you are dating is a healthy choice is to date that person for at least one year prior to engagement. See that person frequently and in every possible circumstance, not just when you both are well rested and ready for a date. See him or her under normal day-to-day living conditions as well. Love grows; infatuation dies. If over time your accumulated experiences are positive and you both feel cared for and cared about, this person may well be a healthy and viable choice for marriage.

Committing yourself to another person may be a scary thought, especially when you seriously consider remarriage. The words of C. S. Lewis seem appropriate and fitting:

> To love at all is to be vulnerable. Love anything, and your heart will certainly be wrung and possibly be broken. If you want to make sure of keeping it intact, you must give your heart to no one, not even to an animal. Wrap it carefully round with hobbies and little luxuries; avoid all entanglements; lock it up safe in the casket or coffin of your selfishness. . . . It will not be broken; it will become unbreakable, impenetrable, irredeemable. . . .

The only place outside Heaven where you can be perfectly safe from the dangers and perturbations of love is
Hell.[3]

This doesn't mean you should take unnecessary risks.
As we have just discussed, there is value in precaution.
But any new step always involves some risk. Risk taking is what causes us to stretch and grow—just make
every attempt to do it wisely. Take the responsibility
because it is your future.

HELPFUL SUGGESTIONS

1. Decide on some principles ahead of time
   that you want to use when you date concerning safety factors, payment for various
   activities, and physical/sexual boundaries.
2. Identify the characteristics and criteria a
   potential partner should meet before you
   begin to date.
3. Have some idea of how often during a week
   or month you want to date a person so you
   can remain objective in assessing that relationship. You may also want to do this so
   you can be available for your other friends
   as well as keeping the door open for other
   potential dating opportunities. Use some
   caution in dating, trust your thoughts and
   feelings, and assess the relationship over a
   long period of time. Write in your journal
   about your experiences as you date. This
   will help you better identify patterns of behavior and evaluate negative and positive
   components.

The Complexities of Remarriage

A second marriage is simply more complex than the first one. There are issues that need to be worked through that did not exist before. That may create some anxiety and apprehension combined with the joy and delight of a new beginning. You definitely are not entirely the same person you were at your first wedding. You most likely have property, a more complex financial life, perhaps children, and other significant relationships. As a result, try to clarify with your prospective partner in what areas you want to maintain some form of separateness and in what areas you will function jointly.

Prenuptial agreements can be extremely helpful. One primary benefit of a prenuptial agreement is that you and your partner disclose to each other your financial status, property, assets, debts, and investments. In any new marriage, money tends to be at the top of the list in issues that create difficulties. In a second marriage, money can become an even greater issue because you accumulated most of your holdings prior to forming this new relationship. Give serious consideration to drawing up a will and a living trust if you have not already done so. You certainly should do this if you have children from your first marriage. You may want to insure that upon your death the assets you accumulated from your first marriage will be protected for the rightful heirs of that marriage rather than being inherited by your second spouse or his or her family.

Discuss thoroughly together how you are going to handle your current incomes when you marry, how you will pay the bills, make purchases, etc. Formulating a budget to show the earnings and projected expenses of both of you can be very reassuring. Also, deciding where you are going to live and how you will financially han-

dle housing is extremely important. If you are not pur-
chasing a new residence but occupying one of your
homes, carefully examine how that will be handled.
Putting the present home into both your names may be
confusing and unfair. Don't be afraid to talk about these
issues and advocate for yourself. This is especially important if the level of income or assets differs significantly between the two of you.

You already have had unfortunate things happen in
your life. What if a few months into your marriage, your
new spouse dies and your finances have not been clearly
arranged? Your newly deceased partner's family may
have an unfair advantage with the inheritance depending on how things were arranged. Make sure that
regardless of what happens to either of you, both of you
will have mutually satisfying arrangements.

Remarriage is indeed a loving and romantic time.
But unlike many first (young) marriages, remarriage at
midlife or later is somewhat like the merger of two major
corporations. Be wise in what you are doing.

Children are another important consideration and
can create complexity in a second marriage. If either
of you have young children or adolescents at home,
the two of you will have to decide who will be primarily responsible for their discipline, what happens
if one parent is not at home, and what the consequences of misbehavior might be. You will want to
address the entire matter of the financial implications
of children, including who will pay for their clothing, activities, lessons, schooling, allowances, and so
on. This may depend to some extent on who earns
the income, the amounts earned, and whose biological children they are. With college-age children you
likely have to face the issues of loans or college tu-
ition payments. If either one of you have grandchil-

dren, you may wish to discuss what level of involvement (if any) you will have financially and/or in the
care of your grandchildren. No matter how uncomfortable you may be in discussing these matters prior
to marriage, they are of utmost importance and cannot be avoided. Discuss them completely until you
and your potential partner have reached agreement
about how to delineate these responsibilities so you
both feel comfortable.

Adult children may have a more difficult time adjusting to a parent's remarriage than younger children
for several reasons:

- They may be concerned about the parent's finances and their potential inheritance later.
- They may be concerned about their place of importance in the surviving parent's life now that
  someone else is in their deceased parent's place.
- They may feel it is disloyal for the surviving parent to replace their deceased mom or dad.
- They may be concerned for their living parent's
  emotional security.
- They have not experienced the new relationship
  as it develops because they are not living with
  their parent on a day-to-day basis.

Bringing a stepparent into the family definitely invades the children's space. Your children do not want
to lose their existing parent, but they will have to deal
with feelings of betrayal to the memory of their deceased parent in moving toward accepting the new person. This certainly means a change for children of all
ages, so spend time with them both by yourself and with
your future spouse, verbally reassuring them that they
will remain important to you and helping them under-

stand how you and your new partner will function in your new marriage. Old family rituals and traditions will need to be revised and adjusted for this new combination of lives. Discuss your marriage plans with your children, and involve them in the wedding. Try to help the children see the benefits of this new relationship and how their lives will be enhanced within this new family constellation.

As a stepparent, you will never replace the children's biological parent. Hopefully that will never be your goal. That doesn't mean you won't be able to have an important and meaningful relationship with them. Be direct, honest, and sensitive to their needs and wants, and show interest in them by talking with them and doing things together.

We have looked at how finances and children can contribute to potential difficulties in remarriage. The third main area of potential conflict is your sexual relationship. One of the primary reasons this area can become a problem is the lack of communication concerning each other's sexual needs and desires. Because you have been married before and have experienced sexual intimacy, you probably have a better idea of who you are sexually and what your desires are. It is wise to discuss these insights together and decide how you will incorporate the similarities and differences into your new marital relationship.

Perhaps you may recognize some weaknesses or regrets you might have had within your first marriage as you discuss sexuality in your new relationship. Try to change these regrets over the past into insights to be incorporated into this new relationship. You have grown through your first marriage; you now have more knowledge and experience you can use the second time around. You have been given another chance not only to begin a new volume in your life but to discover more about your physical and sexual side.

Helpful Suggestions

1. Make certain you and your potential spouse have clearly laid out for each other all of the financial details of your lives, including all assets, debts, income level, retirement and savings plans, and investments. We suggest you do not marry until you have done this together.

2. Jointly write out a financial plan and budget so both of you specifically know how you and your partner will share and handle money management. Also determine how you will divide home management responsibilities as well as the finances of payments and ownership.

3. Determine how you will function with your respective children regarding discipline, money management, decision making, etc. We strongly recommend that you do this together and that you write it down.

4. Evaluate the level of equality and teamwork within your potential marriage. Are you comfortable with this balance? Do you feel significant and equally valued with respect to your choices and opinions? We recommend you write out how decisions will be made when you have conflicting opinions.

5. As a couple, talk with your children concerning their thoughts and feelings (as well as yours) about the coming changes.

Articulate how things will change and in what ways everyone would like to be included in the relationship.
6. Make certain the areas mentioned above are clearly spelled out in an agreeable form. We suggest you draw up a prenuptial agreement in consultation with an attorney.
7. Assess in what area or areas you had realized an inadequacy or desired a change in your first marriage. Discuss this with your new partner to insure that this doesn't repeat itself in your new relationship.

The Other Side of Grief

As you are reading this final chapter, hopefully you are no longer shocked that you are actively living a new life without your deceased spouse. Do you remember thinking after your partner died that the whole world needed to stand still or that you would never feel ready to join with the world that was moving on? You undoubtedly went through a period of time when you were convinced you would never recover from the pain of your grief. But you can move on. Hopefully you are experiencing that right now.

Grief is resolved when the awful pain of grieving is gone. The mourning for the past and for what was is over. You have new hope in your future—a new volume, in whatever form and direction you may choose. How wonderful to be healed! How exciting to stand on the brink of uncharted territory—to begin to dance to a new and different tune. The tune will be different, of course, because you cannot dance to the old music. Your life has changed. The old has passed away and is now stored in your heart and mind in the form of warm, wonderful memories. The new has come, and the new can be very good. Dance, for the new music is beginning.

HELPFUL SUGGESTIONS

1. Celebrate the completion of your difficult and meaningful journey. See this as an occasion to rejoice. Dance—for the mourning is over and you are beginning a new volume.
2. Find opportunities to tell others about your grief journey and its healthy conclusion. In that way you can help educate and change some of the distorted myths that are often held by others who have not had to embark on this journey.

The Pastor Says

Thou hast turned for me my mourning into
dancing;
thou hast loosed my sackcloth
and girded me with gladness,
that my soul may praise thee and not be
silent.
O Lord my God, I will give thanks to thee
for ever.
Psalm 30:11–12 RSV

Mourning into Dancing

When I woke a few days ago, the dawn was overshadowed by thick clouds and fog. Another dreary day.

When you are deep in your grief, each day may seem like that. Even when the sun actually shines, the thick clouds of grief and the fog of despair overshadow any light that might arise.

By midday, however, the clouds began to break. First a little spot appeared here and there. Suddenly the sun broke through, the clouds evaporated, and the temperature warmed. By dinner time, the early spring flowers still damp from the mist were glistening in new sunlight.

In the musical *Annie*, the lead character boasts, "The sun will come out tomorrow." We are not speaking about a simplistic or naive optimism—a fleeting but groundless hope that things might get better. A Christian knows "that in all things God works for the good of those who love him" (Rom. 8:28). This "good" that the Bible promises is not something that will happen only in heaven. This is something God can and will do for us in this life. You do not have to die yourself in order to live again.

So often those who are widowed turn their attention to wondering what life will be like for them in heaven after they die. They imagine they will be reunited with their spouse and again enjoy the companionship and intimacy they once had on this earth. But in the meantime, they wait out the rest of their life stuck in their grief, living with muted emotions. They convince themselves they will never be happy again—at least not until they also die and enter God's eternal joy.

That attitude really has no place in the Christian life. On the contrary, God can turn your mourning into dancing. We are absolutely convinced that in this life God can heal our hurts. He can give grace to our grief and teach us how to live and love again. Surely there are periods of intense grief, pain, and loneliness. But the psalmist says, "Weeping may remain for a night, but rejoicing comes in the morning" (Ps. 30:5). Letting go of your grief is a tremendous challenge, but God can give you the power to let go. The apostle Paul said, "I can do everything through him who gives me strength" (Phil. 4:13). He will give you the power to do what you need to do, and he will empower you in such a way that he also returns joy to your life. Your heart can dance again.

Hopefully you are at a point where you are ready to move on in your life. Even if you are not yet ready to dance again, remember a few things about God and his compassion for you:

1. *God is active daily in your life*. As you reflect on the meditations of this book, remember that God is always near you. His power is ever with you; he will never leave you nor forsake you. When you need to have a reminder of that, read Romans 8 or Matthew 6:25–34, which is the part of the Sermon on the Mount in which Jesus reminds us of God's daily care and concern for us. Sometimes that is hard to remember or recognize. When your husband or wife died, you undoubtedly wondered if God really cared. Does he really have the kind of compassion, love, and tenderness that preachers talk about? Is he as faithful and gracious as the old church hymns portray? But time after time, the Bible tells stories of how God's people suffer in trial after trial only to discover that God really is in control—daily.

2. *God has a good purpose in mind*. The Old Testament uses a special word for *peace*. The word is *shalom*. But the word means much more than just the absence of conflict. *Shalom* means a perfect wholeness, unity, tranquility, and harmony. Shalom is the perfect relationship of all created reality to God the Father and Re-

deemer. Shalom is what Adam and Eve experienced with each other, the world, and with God before they fell into sin. Shalom will come perfectly again when Christ returns, and "he will wipe every tear from their eyes. There will be no more death or mourning or crying or pain, for the old order of things has passed away" (Rev. 21:4). Shalom is the place where the "wolf will live with the lamb" and "the infant will play near the hole of the cobra, yet they will neither harm nor destroy" (Isa. 11:6, 8). This total level of shalom is reserved for the final glory. But God promises peace now, as well. Christ's blessing is always, "Peace I leave with you; my peace I give you. I do not give to you as the world gives. Do not let your hearts be troubled and do not be afraid" (John 14:27).

You know you are getting to the other side of grief when you begin to experience that peace again, when you have a quietness of heart, a sense of contentment and rest that had eluded you during your journey through grief. Remember that Psalm 23 promises that the journey through the valley of the shadow of death emerges into a life in which God's "goodness and love will follow me all the days of my life" (Ps. 23:6). David is not talking about the afterlife—he's not talking about heaven. David is talking about experiencing God's love and goodness in this life for all the rest of your days.

3. *God gives us good along with the evil.* We live in a broken world. As you read Romans 8, pay special attention to verses 22–25. Paul remarks that the "whole creation" is groaning in pain. We are all waiting for redemption—all waiting for that wholeness, or shalom, that God promised. Along with placing our hope in God, we simply have to accept the fact that we do live in a world filled with brokenness. Sickness, pain, and death are symbols of that brokenness. You may think

this sounds simple, but one of the biggest spiritual obstacles to accepting God's power is our own assumption
that God should make things perfect in this world—
here and now. But that simply is not the way God works.
You will get sick; people die of cancer, brain tumors,
and accidents. That's not the way God originally designed it, and that's not the way it will be once Christ
returns. But in the meantime, God says he will give us
strength and hope to live (and die) happily under these
circumstances. And under these circumstances, God
will provide you the strength you need.

Jesus gives us a picture of the Father's love in a story
he told his disciples when explaining the power of
prayer:

> Which of you, if his son asks for bread, will give him a
> stone? Or if he asks for a fish, will give him a snake? If
> you, then, . . . know how to give good gifts to your chil-
> dren, how much more will your Father in heaven give
> good gifts to those who ask him!
>
> Matthew 7:9–11

Without a doubt, you have endured a very difficult
period in your life. Death and its subsequent grief is a
heartrending experience, but God is there in his
strength. He can empower you in the midst of your pain,
and he will give you a new life—a new lease on life—
even before he takes you to your eternal resting place.
God gives us good in the middle of evil.

New Beginnings

Do you know what *sabbath* really means? We often
associate the word with Sunday—a day of rest and worship. But the theme of sabbath is far more rich in Scripture. *Sabbath* really means "new beginnings," and it is in-

tegrally connected with the idea of shalom—that perfect harmonious wholeness God promises.

The biblical pattern of sabbath is a cycle of six plus one. Six days you work, the seventh you rest. In the Old Testament, the Israelites worked the land for six years, but on the seventh year the land would lie fallow. And surprisingly, after seven cycles of seven years, God instructed Israel to return everything to where it was fifty years earlier. All debts were wiped out. Prisoners were to be freed. Land was given back to the family owners. Accumulated wealth was redistributed. They started again.

The Bible gives us new beginnings. Ultimately, of course, the new beginning will be the new heaven and new earth, which Christ will inaugurate with his return. In the meantime, he also lets us begin again. One of the hardest things for me to realize was that the grieving process is also a new beginning. God entrusts us with an opportunity, and we have the responsibility and privilege of using this new beginning wisely. No, we did not ask for it, and we certainly didn't want it. But the new beginning comes.

Instead of resolving to merely make the best of a bad situation, God wants you to move on to recognize that even in the face of death he is giving you a good situation. You truly have a new beginning. You have a chance to reaffirm all that was good in the first volume of your life, but you also have a chance to redo many of the things you may want to do differently. You can begin again. You discover a new sense of self, a new sense of purpose, a deeper relationship with God, and perhaps even a new intimate relationship with another person.

With this new beginning, God can also renew your emotions. Sometimes I looked at the grieving process as a task. Even in our book, we talk about assignments, tasks of grieving, and things we must do. Attending to these matters is important, but God also renews our emotions.

Grief is an extremely powerful emotion, wresting from us tears, terror, and pain, but God can invest us with totally new, positive emotions. The pendulum can swing to the other extreme. My point is simple: Do not avoid the extremes; learn to live on the edges. As great as your grief may have been, so extreme can be your joy. As Christ's Spirit works in you, that Spirit produces fruit in your life. This fruit, listed in Galatians 5:22–23, includes strong emotional overtones. Paul tells us that the Spirit will bring us, among other things, peace, joy, and love. Immerse yourself in God's power, and you will also immerse yourself in powerful, positive emotions. Give yourself the freedom to truly live and love again. When you do that, you have moved to the other side of grief.

We opened this book with a poetic summary of moving to the other side of grief. We invite you to read it again:

Mourning into Dancing

I should dance in God's presence, they say,
though my heart is burdened with grief.

I should revel in God's mercy, they say,
though my life is shattered with pain.

My partner has died.
This is the dark night of my soul.

Days and months press on.
Evenings and mornings lumber past.

My grief is great; my soul cries out,
"Why me, O God? Why me?"

"Not you, my child. Not you.
Your spouse has died. Not you.

I gave you life. I gave you joy.
I can give again."

Sabbath.

Rest now, and begin again.

The sun burns brighter—so slightly brighter.
The pain of the grave becomes the power of grace.

Step by step, God works his miracle.

"You shall dance again, my child.
You shall dance again."

You, O God alone, can turn
My mourning into dancing.

r. de vries

Notes

Chapter 1: Why Grieve?

1. John Bowlby, *Attachment and Loss: Loss, Sadness, and Depression*, vol. 3 (New York: Basic Books, 1980), 96–100.

2. C. S. Lewis, *A Grief Observed* (Greenwich, Conn.: Seabury Press, 1963), 41.

3. Thomas Holmes and Richard Rahe, "The Social Readjustment Ratings Scale," *The Journal of Psychosomatic Research* 2 (1967): 213–18.

4. "Maud Muller," in *John Greenleaf Whittier's Poetry*, ed. Robert Penn Warren (Minneapolis: University of Minnesota Press, 1971), 93.

Chapter 2: How Do You Grieve?

1. Lewis, *Grief Observed*, 7.

2. A number of insightful studies have been conducted on anticipatory grief. See Leon H. Levy, "Anticipatory Grief: Its Measurement and Proposed Reconceptualization," *The Hospice Journal* 7, no. 4 (1991): 1–28; T. A. Rando, ed., *Loss and Anticipatory Grief* (Lexington, Mass.: D.C. Health, 1986); David M. Bass and Karen Bowman, "The Transition from Caregiving to Bereavement: The Relationship of Care-Related Strain and Adjustment to Death," *The Gerontologist* 30, no. 1 (1990): 35–42.

3. Stuart Hample and Eric Marshall, eds., *Children's Letters to God: The New Collection* (New York: Workman Publishing, 1991).

4. Oswald Chambers, *My Utmost for His Highest* (Westwood, N.J.: Barbour and Company, 1963), 120.

5. Richard Foster, *The Freedom of Simplicity* (New York: HarperCollins, 1981), 7.

6. Ibid., 11–12.

7. Ibid., 127.

217

Chapter 3: What Is the Grief Process?

1. One of the earliest proponents of *stage theory* was Elisabeth Kubler-Ross (*On Death and Dying* [New York: Macmillan, 1969]), though technically she addressed the issue of facing terminal illness and not the grief process itself. Sigmund Freud in *Mourning and Melancholia* (London: Hogarth, 1917) was the first to use the term *grief work*, suggesting that a person should intentionally take charge of the grieving process. More recent theories that shift from *stage* to *task* theory are found in Bowlby, *Attachment and Loss*; J. William Worden, *Grief Counseling and Grief Therapy*, 2d ed. (New York: Spring Publishing, 1990); and Colin Murray Parks, *Bereavement Studies of Grief in Adult Life* (New York: International Universities Press, 1972).

2. Wing-Tsit, trans. *The Way of Lao Tzu* (Indianapolis: Bobbs-Merrill Company, 1963), 214.

3. Theresa Rando, *Grief, Dying and Death: Clinical Interventions for Caregivers* (Champaign, Ill.: Research Press, 1984) and *Treatment of Complicated Mourning* (Champaign, Ill.: Research Press, 1993). See also J. William Worden, *Grief Counseling and Grief Therapy*, 2d ed. (New York: Spring Publishing, 1990).

4. Lewis, *Grief Observed*, 49.

Chapter 4: How Can You Take Charge of Your Grief?

1. In addition to this book, you might want to consider reading Carol Staudacher, *A Time to Grieve: Meditations for Healing after the Death of a Loved One* (San Francisco: HarperSanFrancisco, 1994); Melba Colgrove, Harold H. Bloomfield, and Peter McWilliams, *How to Survive the Loss of a Love* (Los Angeles: Prelude Press, 1991); Ruth Coughline, *Grieving: A Love Story* (San Francisco: Harper Perennial, 1994); and Earl A. Grollman, *Living When a Loved One Has Died* (Gilbert, Ariz.: Beacon Press, 1987).

Chapter 5: How Can You Proceed in Your Grief?

1. For additional information about Widowed Persons Services, contact their national headquarters: Widowed Persons Services Programs and Information, c/o AARP (American Association of Retired Persons), 601 E Street, N.W., Washington, D.C. 20049; 202-434-2260.

2. For insights into female sexuality see Lonnie Barbach, *For Yourself: The Fulfillment of Female Sexuality* (New York: Signet, 1976). For male sexuality see Barry and Emily McCarthy, *Male Sexual Awareness: Increasing Sexual Satisfaction* (New York: Carroll and Graf Publishers, 1998). For sexuality in regard to couples see Warwick Williams, *Rekindling Desire: Bringing Your Sexual Relationship Back to Life* (Oakland, Calif.: New Harbinger, 1988).

3. Sidney Zisook and Stephen R. Shuchter, "Early Psychological Reaction to Stress of Widowhood," *Psychiatry* 54 (November 1991): 320–32.

4. Genevieve Ginsburg, *Widow: Rebuilding Your Life* (Tucson: Fisher Books, 1995).

5. John Donne, "Devotions upon Emergent Occasions," section 17, in *The Complete Poetry and Selected Prose of John Donne and the Complete Poetry of William Blake* (New York: The Modern Library, 1941), 332.

Chapter 6: How Does Gender Affect Your Grief?

1. See the discussion of this issue in Ira Glick, Robert Weiss, and Colin Murray Parks, *The First Year of Bereavement* (New York: John Wiley & Sons, 1974); and Sarah Brabant, et al., "Grieving Men: Thoughts, Feelings and Behaviors Following Deaths of Wives," *The Hospice Journal* 8, no. 4 (1992): 33–47.

2. Stephen R. Shuchter and Sidney Zisook, "Treatment of Spousal Bereavement: A Multidimensional Approach," *Psychiatric Annals* 16 (1986): 295–305; and Carol Staudacher, *Men and Grief* (Oakland, Calif.: New Harbinger, 1991).

3. Glick, Weiss, and Parks, *First Year of Bereavement*.

4. Zisook and Shuchter, "Stress of Widowhood," 320–33; and Staudacher, *Men and Grief*.

5. Glick, Weiss, and Parks, *First Year of Bereavement*.

6. Ginsburg, *Widow*; and L. Levy, K. Martin Kouck, and J. Derby, "Differences in Patterns of Adaptation in Conjugal Bereavement: Their Sources and Potential Significance," *Omega* 29, no. 1 (1994): 71–87.

Chapter 7: How Can You Be a Grieving Parent?

1. For smaller children see Leo Buscaglia, *The Fall of Freddie the Leaf* (Thorofare, N.J.: Slack, Inc., 1982); Jill Krementz, *How It Feels When a Parent Dies* (New York: Alfred A. Knopf, 1996); Carol Nystrom, *What Happens When We Die?* (Chicago: Moody Press, 1992); and Earl Grollman, *Talking about Death with Children: A Dialogue between Parent and Child*, 3d ed. (Boston: Beacon Press, 1990). For older children see Hope Edelman, *Motherless Daughters* (New York: Addison-Wesley, 1994); and Earl Grollman, *Bereaved Children and Teens* (Boston: Beacon Press, 1995).

Chapter 8: What about Financial and Employment Issues?

1. Staudacher, *Men and Grief*; and Nini Leick and Marianne Davidson-Nielson, *Healing Pain: Attachment, Loss, and Grief Therapy* (New York: Routledge, 1991).

Chapter 9: What Is the Other Side of Grief?

1. "Comes the Dawn," an anonymous poem cited in Maureen Burns, *Forgiveness: A Gift You Give Yourself* (Greenville, Mich.: Empey Enterprises, 1992), 117.

2. Statistics are from the United States Census Bureau and Adele Nudel, *Starting Over: Help for Young Widows and Widowers* (New York: Dodd, Mead, 1986).

3. C. S. Lewis, *The Four Loves* (New York: Harcourt Brace Jovanovich, 1960), 169.

Index

Susan J. Zonnebelt-Smeenge is a staff psychologist at Pine Rest Mental Health Services, Grand Rapids, Michigan. Her responsibilities include individual, marital, and family psychotherapy; psychological testing; supervision of interns and nonlicensed clinical staff; and clinical coordinator of psychotherapy services at Spectrum Health, Grand Rapids. She is a licensed psychologist, certified social worker, and registered nurse. She is a graduate of Aquinas College and Mercy Central School of Nursing in Grand Rapids and completed advanced studies at Western Michigan University (Ed.D. and M.A. in counseling psychology).

Robert C. De Vries is professor of church education and director of M.A. programs at Calvin Theological Seminary, Grand Rapids, Michigan. He is an ordained pastor in the Christian Reformed Church. He is published in journals and magazines and writes for CRC Publications. He's a graduate of Calvin College and Calvin Theological Seminary, and his advanced degrees include a Ph.D. in adult education from Michigan State University and a D.Min. in church administration from McCormick Theological Seminary, Chicago.

Both authors regularly conduct workshops and speak on grief issues together.